Compiling the Annotated Bibliography

A Guide

Second Edition

Michael J. Eula, Ph.D.
Janet Madden, Ph.D.
El Camino College

KENDALL/HUNT PUBLISHING COMPANY
4050 Westmark Drive   Dubuque, Iowa 52002

Contents

To the Student

For many college students, especially undergraduates, the term *annotated bibliography,* like the concept of the project itself, is unfamiliar. Unlike a research paper, which the student may have been assigned at the secondary level, the annotated bibliography is, by nature of its concentration on scholarship, a collegiate and professional enterprise. The annotated bibliography is a standard research tool and a standard academic assignment used at both the undergraduate and graduate levels.

The purpose of this guide is to provide a theoretical explanation of the project as well as a step-by-step guide for its successful completion. The scholarly articles reprinted in this guide serve as illustrations for the types of articles which you are likely to find in the course of your research for your annotated bibliography project and completing the exercises which follow them will give you valuable experience in finding the main idea, using paraphrase and direct quotes and citing page numbers—the skills you will need for writing the summary portion of your annotated bibliography. The student samples will serve as models for your own research and writing. You will find it helpful to refer to them as you prepare your own work.

About the Annotated Bibliography

What Is an Annotated Bibliography?

A *bibliography* is a list of sources (works consulted and/or cited from) which a writer has compiled as an aid to research. Frequently, the bibliography appears at the end of a research paper in order to demonstrate that the writer has considered the work of others during the construction of a new approach to the topic of the paper.

The *annotated bibliography* differs significantly from a standard bibliography in that the *annotated bibliography* does more than provide the citation for a source (the title of the work, who wrote the work, where and when it was published). The *annotated bibliography* gives the reader a sense of what the work is about; therefore, the *annotated bibliography* is a list of sources with a commentary—the annotation—which appears after the citation for each listed source. The annotation typically does two things: it *summarizes* the main idea of the listed source and it provides a brief *evaluation* of the source's usefulness.

What Is Involved in Compiling an Annotated Bibliography?

Composing the annotated bibliography consists of several parts, or steps, each of which is critical, and each of which involves different skills. It is important to be aware that this is not a project which can be completed quickly; each step will involve a considerable amount of time. Therefore, budgeting your time is probably the most crucial aspect involved in successfully completing this project.

The major steps involved in compiling the annotated bibliography project can be broken down as follows:

1. Identifying a workable research topic.

2. Using library resources to identify, locate, and work with sources that correspond to your topic.

3. Using academic skills to read, summarize, and analyze your sources.

4. Writing summaries and evaluations of each of your sources.

5. Composing the citations, summaries, and evaluations into clear and correct entries and arranging the entries into the completed project.

As you work through this guide, you will learn how to advance through each of these major steps.

What Is the Purpose of the Annotated Bibliography?

The annotated bibliography is a standard academic research tool designed to provide the reader/researcher with a concise guide to titles and contents of research sources. As a *student* at either the undergraduate or graduate level, or, indeed, in your *profession,* you may wish to consult an annotated bibliography for a very important reason: unlike a regular bibliography, which simply provides a list of works on a specific topic, the annotated bibliography provides a commentary on each listed source.

Thus, the annotated bibliography has a great advantage as a research source. It not only allows the reader/researcher to find a prepared list of writings on a specific topic; in addition, it provides an overview of the material contained in each source while also providing a sense of the usefulness of that material. The amount of time and energy that a researcher can save by consulting an annotated bibliography makes this a uniquely valuable research tool.

As the *compiler* of an annotated bibliography, you will gain invaluable experience of planning and conducting serious and sustained library research on an academic topic. Even more important, the annotated bibliography allows you to pursue a primary goal of a college education—serious scholarly reading on a topic of interest to you.

Because you must summarize the contents of your sources, you will be able to demonstrate your understanding of sources. In your evaluatory comments, you will have the opportunity to respond critically to the scholarship you have read. Finally, because an annotated bibliography treats each source separately, you are not asked to integrate various approaches and arguments to your topic in essay form. Instead, your task is to engage in a concentrated internal dialogue with each source. The annotated bibliography, therefore, is a *learning experience* which gives you the freedom to engage in meaningful *research* but does not ask you to take a professional stance which you have not as yet attained.

What Is the Difference Between an Annotated Bibliography and a Research Paper?

Many students, especially those who have been conditioned to associate a research project with the writing of a term paper, research essay, or research paper, initially have some trouble in conceptualizing the scope and purpose of the annotated bibliography project.

Unlike a research paper, the annotated bibliography does *not* ask you to synthesize research and attempt to conduct an argument of your own. Instead, the annotated bibliography might best be considered a *"pure"* research project. While you will conduct serious academic library research—in fact, you may spend far *more* time conducting research for an annotated bibliography project than for a conventional research paper—you will spend most of your time engaging in academic reading. While this academic reading and research is work most central to the college experience, the reality of a college education is that college courses frequently focus the student's attention on textbooks rather than on the actual practice of a discipline. The professor who assigns an annotated bibliography is choosing to direct the student to scholarship in the relevant field and is therefore indicating a desire to expose the student to the practice of scholarship within a particular academic discipline.

When Might You Be Assigned an Annotated Bibliography?

Many college courses, both at the undergraduate and at the graduate level, require students to compile an annotated bibliography instead of writing a research paper. There are a number of reasons why your professor might choose the annotated bibliography assignment over the research paper: the primary reason is that the annotated bibliography project allows the student to engage in serious, sustained academic research and to engage in what becomes virtually an independent study project within the larger parameters of the course of study.

Many college students find writing a research paper a meaningless exercise in patching together quotations from various sources. Often, students feel this way because they have been assigned to write a paper on a topic that they know nothing about, and the multiple tasks of research, synthesis, and conducting an independent argument begin to seem like an attempt to pass oneself off as a expert. The work involved in compiling an annotated bibliography project is no less rigorous than that involved in the writing of a research paper. But one advantage of the annotated bibliography over the research paper is that the annotated bibliography allows the student to become steeped in the scholarly literature relating to the selected topic. For this reason, a number of college professors believe that undergraduate students, in particular, benefit significantly from the experience of the annotated bibliography project. They believe that students need the opportunity to acquire a basic grounding in library research practices and in the scholarly literature of the field of study *before* they are asked to engage in the sustained scholarly argument that underpins a research paper.

What Is the Value of the Annotated Bibliography?

Above all, the annotated bibliography is the student's opportunity to become immersed in scholarship—to have the time to really understand various viewpoints of experts in the field—even viewpoints that sometimes conflict. In addition to serving as a valuable research project in its own right, the annotated bibliography project can serve as the basis for a research paper. It can, in fact, be publishable in and of itself. Or it can serve as the basis for a longer, more sustained bibliography and/or research paper in the future.

Steps in Writing an Annotated Bibliography

Selecting a Topic

The first rule of thumb in selecting a topic is making sure that you choose something which fits within the parameters of the course you are taking. If you are taking a course in History 1A—The History of the United States to 1877, for example, you cannot select a topic such as "Economic Consequences of the Great Depression" because this topic clearly falls outside the limits of the course. Similarly, if you are enrolled in English 15A—Survey of English Literature from Beowulf to Swift, you may not choose a topic such as "Yeats' love poetry." If, after attempting to ascertain whether or not a topic falls within the purview of the course, you are still in doubt about whether a topic is acceptable, check with your professor. Use the Project Registration form at the end of this Guide to formally register your project if your professor requires such registration.

The second rule in selecting a topic is making sure that you have some interest in the subject about which you choose to write. If you are having difficulty in selecting a topic, try the obvious—look through lecture notes, skim the index of a text you are using for the course, check an existing bibliography on a topic included in the material for your course. These are all ways to generate ideas. Again, if in any doubt, you should be sure to get feedback from your professor.

Finding Scholarly Sources

In every academic discipline, much of the newest work and research can be found not in books, but in recent *scholarly articles*. When you think about it, the reason is obvious: books take longer to prepare and publish than articles do. Articles in journals or magazines, however, because they are shorter and focused more specifically on a narrower topic, can be produced more quickly. For reasons of currency within a field, professors may specify that you are to use *scholarly articles* rather than books in preparing your annotated bibliography.

Many students have difficulty in understanding the difference between *scholarly* (academic) and non-scholarly, or *general,* sources. The basic difference between the two is that *scholarly* articles provide footnotes, endnotes, and/or a bibliography. You will not find scholarly articles suitable for use in an annotated bibliography in general publications such as *Newsweek, National Geographic, Mother Jones, American History Illustrated,* or *Rolling Stone.* Usually, publications suitable for use in the annotated bibliography assignment will have titles such as *English Literary History, The Journal of Social History,* or *PMLA (Publications of the Modern Language Association).* One way to visually understand the difference between general and scholarly publications is to take a few moments to look at the current periodicals (magazines and journals) on display in the Periodicals Room of the Library. You will quickly see the difference between *American History Illustrated* and *American Historical Review.* The two scholarly articles published in this Guide are typical of those published in academic journals.

Using Indices

In order to conduct scholarly research in periodical sources, you will need to use the standard indices available in a college or university library. Various academic disciplines are indexed in different indices, of course, so you should be careful about which index you use. It is very important to remember that you will *not* find scholarly sources listed in *The Reader's Guide to Periodical Literature.* This is because this index lists only general (popular, not scholarly) publications. For the same reason, you do not want to use newspaper indices for this assignment. Instead, you need to discover which indices will provide the kind of scholarly articles you need. Standard computerized scholarly indices include the following: *MLA* (for articles on literature); *Social Science Index* (for disciplines within the social sciences); *Humanities Index* (for literature, history, the arts, and related topics); *Academic Index* (for various academic disciplines). These are the largest and most inclusive of the standard academic periodical indices. There are also, of course, other, smaller, narrower indices. Obviously, the more the index is focused on a discipline, the easier it will be to find what you want from it. This is where consulting the periodicals or reference librarian as to what index will best serve your purpose and will save you a great deal of time and energy. The number of sources you need will, of course, depend on the number of articles that you have been assigned to locate, summarize, and evaluate.

As you locate and photocopy articles, be sure that you at least *skim the contents* to be sure that the articles will fit in with your overall topic; titles can sometimes be deceptive. In fact, it may be a good idea to locate more articles than you will actually need, in case one or two sources turn out not to be available. If you are using a computerized index, the computer entry for the article will tell you whether or not the library in which you are working carries that journal you need. Remember to check the library's periodicals holdings list to find out whether your library has the *date* as well as the *title* of the journal that you need. Acquiring articles from journals not held in the library in which you are working may require you to visit another library or use inter-library loan services. Check with the reference or periodicals librarian if you find yourself in this position. Consult the *Serials* list (held at the reference or the periodicals desk) for information on journal holdings in other libraries.

Above all, be sure that you **write down all citation information that you will need** as your research proceeds, keeping in mind that you will need to write a correct citation for each source. It is always far more work to go back through the research process searching for a missing piece of information than to make sure that you have all the information you need while you are still in the research stage. A good way to make sure that you have all necessary information is to write the necessary information *in correct citation form* (see the section on *Types of Citations* for more information) at the top of each photocopied source. Take this Guide with you to the library as you do research. Take special care to find out whether your source paginates by *volume* or by *issue*—if you are using MLA citation form.

Types of Citations

The standard citation form for books is very straightforward; MLA, for example, looks like this:

Eula, Michael. *Between Peasant and Urban Villager: Italian-Americans of New Jersey and New York, 1880–1980. The Structures of Counter-Discourse.* New York: Peter Lang, 1993.

Madden, Janet. *Woman's Part. An Anthology of Short Fiction By and About Irish Women, 1890–1960.* London: Marion Boyars, 1983.

As you can see, for **MLA** style (be aware that this is only **one** style; you may be required to use a different one, such as **APA** or **Chicago**) you need to be sure that you alphabetize entries by last name, that you indent each line following the first line of the entry, and that you follow the order as above. However, if your professor requires you to use only scholarly articles and does not allow you to use books in compiling your annotated bibliography, then you must the citation forms which are appropriate for journal articles. A further point to keep in mind is that different disciplines use different citation forms. For the Humanities and the Social Sciences, the standard forms are the: *MLA* (The Modern Language Association of America; Literature); *APA* (American Psychological Association; Social Sciences); *AHA/Chicago* (History). This Guide contains only journal citation forms; for complete information for every type of citation, you will need to consult the relevant style manual produced by the individual academic discipline. Keep in mind that the form you use will depend on the discipline in which you are working. *It is very important that you make sure which form your professor wants you to use.*

Sample MLA Citation Form for Journals (Literature)

There are two types of MLA citation forms for journals. The distinction between the two turns on how the journal is paginated. One form is *pagination by volume* (sometimes called continuous pagination); the other is *pagination by issue* (also called separate pagination).

Pagination by Volume

Some journals continue page numbers throughout the year instead of beginning each issue with page 1. Then, at the end of the year, all of the issues are collected into a volume. To find an article in the journal, the reader needs to know the *volume number,* the *year* and the *page numbers* of an article.

Kirsch, Arthur. "Macbeth's Suicide." *ELH* 51 (1984): 269–296.

Pagination by Issue

Some journals begin each issue of the journal with page 1. If this is the case with the journal you are using, you need to indicate the number of the issue. To do so, put a period after the number of the volume and follow it with the number of the issue.

Hester, M. Thomas. "A Preface to the Reader of Donne's Lyrics." *Christianity and Literature* 39.4 (1990): 365–85.

Sample APA Citation Form for Journals (Psychology)

Like MLA, APA distinguishes between pagination by volume and pagination by issue. However, APA citation style differs significantly from MLA. For example, authors' initials are used instead of first names. The date appears in parentheses immediately after the author's name. Do not place the title of articles in quotation marks. An entry is not indented, although any line after the first is indented three spaces.

Pagination by Volume

Rowe, G.S. (1989). Black Offenders, Criminal Courts, and Philadelphia Society in the late Eighteenth-Century. *Journal of Social History,* 62, 685–712.

Pagination by Issue

McMillen, Sally. (1985). Mothers' Sacred Duty: Breast-Feeding Patterns among Middle- and Upper-Class Women in the Antebellum South. *The Journal of Southern History,* 60 (3), 334–56.

Sample AHA/Chicago Form for Journals (History)

This citation format does not distinguish between journals paginated by volume and those paginated by issue. In AHA/Chicago style, the first line is indented 5–7 spaces. The title of the article appears in quotation marks. The abbreviation "pp." indicates pages. The month or season precedes the date; notice that there is no punctuation between the month/season and the year.

AHA/Chicago Journal Citation

Bailey, Samuel L. "The Adjustment of Italian Immigrants in Buenos Aires and New York, 1870–1914." *American Historical Review.* April 1983, pp. 281–305.

Writing Your Annotated Bibliography

How to Write a Summary

The summary is the major part of each annotated bibliography entry. How long it should be depends, in part, on what your professor expects of you. Be sure to have a clear idea of the expected length in mind *before* you begin to write. The summary demonstrates your understanding of the article you have researched and read. Essentially, the summary is a condensed version of the scholarly piece that you have read, and the most important part of your summary is your ability to locate and express the *main idea* of the piece of writing that you are summarizing. In order to accomplish this aim, you must be able to distinguish between main ideas and minor ones, and between larger theoretical assertions and specific support. The good summary has three outstanding features:

It is *brief.*

It is *objective.*

It is *clear.*

By its nature, the summary cannot replicate every point made in the article you have read. Your job is essentially that of translator—in *your own words and your own sentence structure,* you will *restate* the ideas of the writer, and you will do so clearly, briefly, and objectively. There is *no* room in the summary for your opinion—save your thoughts for the evaluatory comment which will follow it.

Following these steps **in the order listed** will help you to write a good summary:

1. Read the article carefully, so that you can answer the following questions:

   A. What is the *topic* of the article?

   B. What is the writer's *purpose* in writing the article (for example, is the writer conducting an argument, trying to persuade the reader, analyze something, compare two events or writings?)

   C. What is the writer's *main point*? Locate and underline or highlight the *major ideas, minor points,* and *supporting ideas or examples.*

2. Go back and reread the article, noticing how the author proceeds from introduction to conclusion. Pay special attention to *organization.* Notice how the author uses paragraphs; pay attention to any labeled subheadings within the article. You may wish to write notes to yourself in the margins of the article as you work through the article's ideas and examples.

3. Write a one-sentence **restatement of the main idea of the article in your own words.** Although it is not obligatory, it is usual to identify the author by *full name* in this sentence. Subsequent references to the author are by *last name only.*

4. Now you are ready to *draft* your summary. As you write, be sure to include only information you consider important; because a summary must be concise, you will not have room to include minor details.

5. When you have completed the draft, you are ready to *revise.* Be sure that you have included all major ideas. Insert *transitions* to make your sentences smoother, and make sure that your sentences are smooth and that you do not unnecessarily repeat information. You may incorporate *quotations* from the article as appropriate; if you do use quotations, limit quoted material to key *words* or *phrases.* Be sure to enclose them in quotation marks and also be sure that they fit smoothly into the sentences in which they appear. Indicate the pages from which they are taken by the use of parenthetical reference; see the student sample in the guide. The final step in the revision stage is checking for correct grammar, punctuation, and spelling. Be sure that you have written your summary in the correct

tense. As you will notice from looking at the student samples provided in this Guide, you must write in the *present tense* (the author *argues,* the writer *points out,* Eula *contends*).

6. When you have revised your summary, read it over to check that it fulfills the most basic function of any summary: be sure that reading your summary would provide someone who had not read the scholarly article with a clear and correct idea of its contents.

How to Write an Evaluation

The evaluatory comment which follows the summary is your chance to comment on the article you have researched, read, and summarized. You may wish to use the evaluatory comment to discuss the author's writing style. Or, you may wish to comment on the merits of the argument conducted in the article. You may wish to express your personal response to the topic of the article, the point of view expressed by the author, or the quality of support the writer provides. As you will see from the student samples included in this Guide, the evaluatory comment is substantially shorter than the summary. Like the summary, the evaluatory comment is written in the present tense. The point to remember here is that the evaluatory comment is the exact opposite of the summary—in the summary you *cannot* express your personal opinion, but in the evaluatory comment, you *must* express your personal opinion.

Putting Your Project Together

When you have completed the citation, summary and evaluative comment for each of your entries, you are ready for the *compilation* phase of your annotated bibliography. The number of entries, of course, will depend on how many entries have been assigned by your professor. Organized in alphabetical order according to the last name of the author, each entry should begin on at the top of a new sheet of paper. Each page should have a running head (your last name and the page number of your project). Finally, attach the cover sheet provided at the end of this Guide so that it is the first page of your project. Remember that it is *always* wise to make a copy of any assignment before submitting it for a grade.

Sample Scholarly Articles

Reading the two scholarly articles that follow will give you practice in recognizing and reading academic writing. You should use these articles to practice your ability to locate the main idea and major supporting ideas of the article.

Answering the study questions that follow each article will help to prepare you for your independent research and writing.

"Cultural Continuity and Cultural Hegemony: Italian Catholics in New Jersey and New York, 1880–1940" appeared in the journal *Religion,* volume 22, in 1992, pages 327–348.

"*Miss Erin:* Nationalism, Feminism, and the Popular 19th Century Anglo-Irish Novel" appeared in the journal *Eire-Ireland* Volume XXV, Number 1, in Earrach-Spring, 1990, pages 106–112.

Cultural Continuity and Cultural Hegemony: Italian Catholics in New Jersey and New York, 1880–1940

Michael J. Eula

In this essay I trace the theological continuity evident in Italian Catholic traditions. This line of continuity has its immediate historical origins in the religious forms of Italian rural folk. Those practices were then taken to New Jersey and New York in the closing decades of the 19th century, where they remained in evidence until well into the 20th century. The emotional configuration of the peasant in a traditional society remained as the emotional configuration of the Italian-American worker. The way in which peasants contextualized their theological lives in rural Italy was similar to the way they did so in America, for in the latter, as in the former, class subordination remained a central reality of daily life. Despite that subordination, peasants and workers achieved an air of dignity through the construction of Catholic practices which served to undermine further attempts to implement ideological domination.

> Entering and exiting. Those two words should be abolished. One does not enter or exit; one continues.
>
> Antonio Gramsci, in *Avanti!* (1917)

Introduction

The religious culture of Italian Catholics has been consciously perpetuated as a distinct view of a subordinate class. Accordingly, the subservient attitudes associated with this view lessened the effect of mobility won from generation to generation. At the end of the 19th century, Southern Italy, still a traditional society, was characterized by a culture in which social mobility, if it occurred at all, was so slow as to remain almost undetectable. When the peasants left southern Italy for New Jersey and New York, they brought traditional emotional patterns along with them "in the baggage" to a liberal, capitalist America. Producing a pattern unique to the northeastern United States but not to rural Italy, these peasants continued their Old World patterns of class subordination. Over time, the reality of the class structure combined with demographic concentration to produce a working class culture replete with emotional characteristics similar to those evident in rural Italy.[1]

But Roman Catholicism played a remarkable role in this new situation. From the perspective of the subordinate class, it constituted a force poised against domination. The Catholicism of the peasants was more than a simple

16

retreat into the privacy of the heart. Catholicism became in fact an important component of the active social role in which a subordinate class engages. The political passivity which the peasants periodically revealed seldom affected their religion. The central qualities of their religious world remained one of their own making. In the process, it was used to assert class dignity.

The Catholicism of Italian peasants offered a diverse assortment of rites and public ceremonies. It was a ritualized, spontaneous religion of resistance. It made no pretense of being theologically rigorous and rejected most attempts on the part of the Catholic hierarchy to systematize belief. Indeed, many 19th-century Catholic rituals continued to be grounded in ancient customs predating Catholicism. Religion thrived as a spontaneous force invoking the supernatural against forces of arbitrary domination.

In novelist Giovanni Verga's 1880 publication of *The She-Wolf* we are given a fictional illustration of how Christian customs combined with pre-Christian beliefs to ward off evil.[2] The Christian rites, which Verga describes, are in reality, manifestations of these pre-Christian beliefs. The sign of the cross, for example, becomes not only a means of expressing reverence; rather, it is a defensive strategy designed to ward off the She-Wolf's evil. Nor does the priest occupy his proper place in the Christian social order. Though ordained by the Church as a minister of the sacraments whose primary responsibility was the care of souls, Verga's account informs us that peasants regarded the priest as unable to care for his own soul—not to mention the souls of others. Such views point to the profound gap between the Church's version of Christianity and that of the peasantry. The peasants saw the Church not as a representative of God's kingdom, but rather, as little more than another tool in their arsenal—one among a repertoire of strategic devices to counter arbitrary dominance. The peasants regarded Church leaders as part of that manipulative array that served to make their life a hard one. As a result, the gulf between church leaders and the local populace was not easily bridged. Priests on the local level understood this better than their superiors. This led to deep apathy among the Church authorities, which such observers as Luigi Villari noted in his 1902 publication of *Italian Life in Town and Country*.[3]

The unification of Italy by 1871 served to change the peasant's relation to the Church—but only superficially. Before unification, the hierarchy of the Church, including that of the priests, was composed almost entirely of members of the elite. This collection of titled nobles, courtiers, and university-trained intellectuals did not attempt to appeal to the peasantry in their own terms. The very language of the Mass—Latin—was one peasants did not usually comprehend. The rigidity of official Catholicism stood in stark contrast to the rich amalgam of Catholic and pre-Christian religion practiced by the new arrivals in America. The social distance between hierarchy and peasantry only solidified.

This social distance was also widened by inequities in the control of communal property. In the years before unification, material benefits distributed within the framework of traditional society lessened peasant suspicion of elite culture. In traditional society, the Church played a leading role as a benefactor to the poor. Roman law still dictated, until 1861, that Church lands were also public lands, and as such were subject to the legal authority of local municipalities. Municipal officials were thus obliged by law to uphold the distinction between public land traditionally held by the Church and administered by the municipality on the one hand and, on the other hand, the domains of the princes and their rights to private land.[4] In effect, the Church was part of a legal tradition that extended back at least to the 2nd century. Central to this tradition was the principle of "usufruct," a crucial benefit in the daily life of the peasant. Alan Watson has succinctly defined this principle as "the right to use and enjoy the fruits of another's property but not to alter its character fundamentally or destroy it." The elite, through the institution of the Church, lived up to its conservative role as social leader by providing the peasant access to public land. Here the peasant was able, for example, to hunt and forage for wood. But it should also be remembered that the peasant never forgot that this "right" was a privilege which could be revoked.[5] Indeed, as one scholar notes, "the Church never asked permission or the endorsement of the peasant whenever it chose to build a new covent or a monastery."[6] Such structures served to limit the amount of acreage available to the peasants. Their access to public lands, while beneficial, nevertheless drove home the constant presence of a personal vulnerability rooted in a clearly subordinate social position.

In the years after unification, land reform hit the Church particularly in the south. The newly constituted central government enacted a series of land reforms that, by 1880, resulted in the privatization of at least one million acres.[7] A major source of wealth was rapidly slipping away from the Church. Peasants who had traditionally relied upon public lands suddenly found themselves illegally trespassing on private lands owned by barons and a rising middle class.[8]

Land reform had a profound effect on the peasant perception of the Church. The alien culture of priests with elite backgrounds had been tolerated because it had granted access to public lands. With these benefits now lost, the bonds between the Church and the peasantry slackened. As the Church rapidly became impoverished, so too did its ranks of priests. Not surprisingly, during the first two decades after the completion of Italian unification, the privileged departed from the priesthood in unprecedented numbers, although they still remained in the higher echelons of the Church hierarchy.[9] Priests recruited from the lower social classes, i.e., the artisans and the peasantry, were rapidly replacing them.[10] But instead of bringing the Church closer to its parishioners it had, surprisingly, just the opposite effect. Peasants had deferred to the priest who was a member of the elite. The control which those priests exercised over public lands reinforced deference. Impoverished priests, however, exercised no such authority over lands that were in any event private. Both Church and peasantry grew increasingly poor. Poor priests and monks, who still retained the stigma of lower class origins, were forced to go through the village as beggars. Benefactors had become little more than street urchins. What deference remained by the late 19th century was based, as much as anything else, on personal factors such as the fear of the priest's curse. One immigrant from the village of Ventimiglia in Calabria recalled that:

> There were three churches with three priests. Besides there was a duomo (cathedral) that was connected with a monastery on the outskirts of town. Some of the one hundred or so monks performed duties as priests or as teachers in the local school. The majority of them did begging, going from village to village and from house to house. People hated these parasites but were afraid to refuse them a donation because these holy men could curse one's crop or bring about some other misfortune.[11]

This Calabrian peasant's perspective was not unique in Southern Italy. Likewise, as we will now see, it was evident in New Jersey and New York as well.

Arrival in America

Italian peasant religion did not easily lend itself to the development of an autonomous individual who, through the exercise of initiative, could embrace a success that was both material and spiritual. Yet this was precisely a central assumption of the Irish-American Catholic hierarchy greeting Italian peasants in New Jersey and New York at the beginning of the 20th century. The writings of the contemporary Catholic observer Paul V. Flynn tell us much in this regard. In his description of Catholic education in Newark at the end of the 19th century, he depicts a link between self-initiative and spiritual devotion that differed little from the Protestant work ethic of the era.[12] He argues that poor Irish children had risen to places of prominence in Newark because of their hard work and spiritual immersion in Catholic doctrine. Like other Christians of that era, Flynn's Catholic combined the initiative of economic man with a spiritually fostered attack upon the baser side of human nature.

Southern Italian peasants, both before and after their arrival in America, never quite understood this relationship between Christian ethics and the imperatives of a marketplace. Their religion did not endorse the proliferation of subjective and, at least ideally, autonomous moral demands. Rather, in a pattern described by such scholars as John Bossy, it sanctioned an array of intervening saints whom they believed afforded the individual protection against capricious and arbitrary enemies.[13] Within such a framework, subjective guides to behavior had no place. Religion for southern Italian peasants was fundamentally conservative—the history of the individual was a series of tactical defensive maneuvers. Spiritual devotion never led to a better world, either on earth or beyond. This perspective was brought whole and entire to New Jersey and New York, where it clashed not only with the liberalism of Protestantism, but also, with the systematic and hopeful optimism of the Catholic Church.

The conflict encouraged an ever widening gap between the Church and Italian-Americans in New Jersey and New York throughout the early 20th century. The American Church, dominated by an educated and nationalistic Irish-American clergy, wielded a power that was not seriously challenged through to 1940. To the Irish-American churchman, the Catholic Church was his. It was a church with strong political roots in the resistance against British imperialism in Ireland.[14] It had sustained Irish immigrants in a hostile Protestant America, serving as a central institution in the forging of a strong group identity devoid of the regionalism so prevalent among Italians.

Along with the sheer numerical dominance of the Irish, there was again the issue of theological doctrine. Just as in Italy, the Church in America engaged in a constant battle with popular religious forms. But the Irish-American hierarchy had no experience with the popular Catholicism unique to Italian peasants. And they were not about to accept it into their church. Thus, in comparison to Italian peasant theology, Irish Catholicism's systematic and rigid qualities appeared even more pronounced. With an emphasis upon the supremacy of God and focus upon Jesus as the primary object of worship, there was no place for the myriad of deities which abounded in the Italian religious construct. Horrified Irish priests discovered that the Catholicism of Italian immigrants relegated God and Jesus to a secondary position. "Unlike their Irish Catholic neighbors," a Rochester Italian-American remarks, Italians "had almost no fear of God and felt as much at home with him as they did with each other."[15] Such perspectives troubled the Irish-American clergy. In 1913 a writer in the *Ecclesiastical Review,* commenting on Italian immigrants, argued that "religious indifference is a ravaging contagion among them. . . ."[16] A priest out of New York's Nativity Church adds that:

> the Italians are not a sensitive people like our own. When they are told that they are about the worst Catholics that ever came to this country, they don't resent it or deny it. If they were a little more sensitive to such remarks they would improve faster. The Italians are callous as regards religion.[17]

Flynn laments that "it is unfortunate . . . that so many of the men are so luke-warm, indifferent to the practices of their religion." He then refers to a common subject of Irish-Catholic critique. The men, he observes, "are seemingly content-ed to have their wives and daughters do all the praying."[18]

From the Irish perspective, Italian immigrants posed a clear theological threat. To a clergy and lay people steeped in the absolute authority of God and Jesus, the Italian system of saints seemed incomprehensible. So too did the pop-ular forms of religion among southern Italians, which included informal masses, feasts with dubious Christian links, and strict separation between the public reli-gious duties of men and women. Most threatening of all, from the Irish point of view, was the tendency of Italian-Americans to dismiss priests who insisted upon strict interpretations of Catholic doctrine. As Flynn remarks:

> some seem to think that they may at will discharge the Priest whom the Bishop has sent to them and supplant him with another of their selection. Shortly after the Mission was opened, no less than three Italian priests were invited by their countrymen to come to Newark. These people would like a church edifice, to do with it as they please. . . .[19]

Not surprisingly, antipathy quickly dominated Irish-Italian relations in the Church. Continuously stunned by what they perceived as disrespect for the Church and even for God, Irish clergy, and their followers, commented bitterly on the "heathen" quality of Italian Catholic worship. As a result of such appraisals, Italian-Americans became what the historian Alberto Giovannetti called "basement Catholics." In 1886, one immigrant said that "we Italians were allowed to worship only in the basement part of the church" at East 115th Street in East Harlem. Other documents of the period, such as the *Souvenir History of Transfiguration Parish—Mott Street*, New York, 1827–1897, reveal the sharp distinction between the "upper" and "lower" Catholic church:

> While all that we have spoken refers to the upper church, let it not be forgotten that we have three Masses in the basement for the Italians of the parish, and that Father Ferretti, under Father McLoughlin's direction, does very efficient work for that portion of his flock.[20]

Theological differences that led to this sort of discrimination intensified the conflict between Italian immigrants and the Irish-American church in an unex-pected way. A small but vocal number of immigrants began to break completely with Catholicism. Irish clergy had not cultivated the spirit of theological com-promise evident in rural Italian villages, where the Church viewed an outward form of Catholicism as better than no Catholicism at all. Continued insistence on assigning Irish priests to Italian neighborhoods, along with a failure to recognize the legitimacy of popular religious rites, drove some immigrants to desperate measures. From their perspective, complete secession appeared to be the only option.

Solutions

In 1914 "The Independent National Roman Catholic Church of St. Anthony of Padua" was formed in Hackensack, New Jersey. In a privately published history written in 1962, Father Joseph Anastasi tells of the Italian-Americans who were denied a church of their own by the Irish-dominated hierarchy in Newark.[21] "They petitioned the Bishop of the Roman Catholic Diocese of Newark to send them an Italian priest to organize an Italian parish," Anastasi explains, "but their request was not granted." He adds that "a petition was repeated time and again, and each time it was met with the same denial by the Roman Hierarchy; St. Mary's Church was good enough."[22]

After months of fruitless petitioning to the Bishop, a young priest at Our Lady of Mount Carmel church in Newark, Father Giulio Lenza, entered the strife. An assistant pastor frustrated by his lack of responsibility at Mount Carmel, and disturbed by the Irish hierarchy's treatment of Italian-Americans, Lenza was also a political populist. He began to travel frequently to Hackensack in an effort to persuade "the people to organize their own Italian parish in spite of the Bishop's refusal." He was confident that "such action would force the Bishop's hand and, if necessary, the case could be presented to the Apostolic Delegate in Washington and to the Holy Father in Rome." We are told that the "whole colony rallied to him." Thus, during the Christmas season of 1914, St. Anthony of Padua was "incorporated under the State Law."[23]

The reaction of the Church in Newark and Washington was swift and sure. Anastasi recalls that:

> the Roman Bishop of Newark was not to take all of this with a smile. The adventurer priest was "ipso facto" suspended and another priest was dispatched to Hackensack to organize a bona fide Roman parish among the Italians of the First Ward. A letter from the Apostolic Delegate in Washington, denouncing the suspended priest as an impostor, was freely circulated and all the Italians were urged to support the priest sent to them by the Bishop and to have nothing to do with Father Lenza.[24]

After struggling for years with debts and the "hate and antagonism" of local Catholics who remained loyal to the Church, St. Anthony's eventually re-emerged under the auspices of the Episcopal Church. Unlike the Catholic Church in Hackensack, the Episcopalians made numerous concessions to the popular religious rites of Italian immigrants. Interested only in "our Lord's lost sheep," the Episcopalians undertook such an array of accommodations that "the people of St. Anthony's were fully convinced of the Catholicity of the Episcopal church and of the validity of her Sacraments."[25]

This spirit of independence among Italian Catholics became a concern among some of the lesser Irish clergy from the early 1880s on. Unlike their superiors who had far less contact with Italian immigrants, these clergymen were concerned about the Italian propensity for independence. They thus mounted a campaign within the hierarchy which called for compromises with popular religion.[26] Incidents like the one in Hackensack were occurring with alarming regularity. The intransigence of the Irish hierarchy continued to be met with Italian rebellion throughout the New York metropolitan area. A letter from a local pastor to Bishop Wigger in Newark characterizes the warnings emanating from the local level:

> The contagious fever of building private chapels . . . by the Italians in Hoboken is on the increase. Another son (T. Damelio), a good man taken by this kind of spirit, is building another chapel on his own private property, and at his own private expense.[27]

This outbreak of rebelliousness, along with the conversion of a minority of Italian-Americans to evangelical religions, eventually convinced the Irish hierarchy that some compromises were called for.[28] What we see, then, is an eventual adoption of the attitude visible in the Roman Catholic Church of Italy—the outward form of Catholicism is better than no Catholicism at all. Even a Catholicism replete with popular religious rites was superior to the spectacle of Italian immigrants wandering into such institutions as the Broome Street Tabernacle or the Brooklyn City Mission. Evangelical preachers were increasingly capitalizing on the alienation and anger felt by some Italian-Americans towards the Catholic Church. Working on a daily basis in the ethnic communities, ministers were able to see what local Irish priests were warning about. In Albany the Reverend Creighton R. Story of the First Baptist Church noted that:

> We have made some gratifying discoveries, some of which might be mentioned. First of all, the Italians are not such loyal Romanists as we supposed. some of them are, but the majority have nothing but indifference or aversion for the whole extortionate and oppressive system . . . They are most susceptible to sympathy; they do not desire alms but Christian friendliness.[29]

Irish clergy thus began mounting a counterattack on the intrusion of evangelicals through a concerted accommodation with southern Italian religion. As early as 1899, such churches as Our Lady of Mount Carmel in Newark were known for their "Italian ways and traditions, such as the celebration of certain Italian patron saint feast days." "Diocesan authorities acquiesced here," we were told, "as they had at St. Peter and Paul in Hoboken."[30] Acquiescence translated into a reluctant toleration of popular religious rites which the Irish hierarchy continued to disdain.[31] That toleration, however, differed fundamentally from the kind evident in Italy. In New Jersey and New York, Irish-American church leaders insisted on a clear theological division between popular forms and Catholic doctrine. Irish priests continued to advocate the rigid and impersonal theology of the Church while ignoring such manifestations of southern Italian theology as the feast. Italian communities were eventually allowed to construct their churches—but they tempered their resentment with a realization that the Church was making compromises. However, few knew just what some of "their" Italian priests thought of them. In 1903, Father Gideon de Vincentitis wrote to the Pope from New Jersey:

> Your Holiness, we earnestly beg you to save us that shame which more than any other causes us Italian priests to blush. This terrible and glaring ignorance of our people makes us the butt of sarcastic depreciation. It is our real cross in America.[33]

Italian-American workers, typically ignorant of what their spiritual leaders really thought, were satisfied with the concessions won by the beginning of the 20th century. They went out happily to live those victories which, they were convinced, made them no less Catholic than their Irish superiors.

The first signs of victory for those popular rites (not yet tolerated within the confines of the American Catholic church) were apparent in the 1880s. Numerous observers noted the initiative taken by immigrants in fostering their traditions without benefit of the Church's approval.[34] "Nominally, they are all Roman Catholics," a writer in *The Cosmopolitan* discovered, "but as a class they are very little attracted to that organization." Accordingly, Italian immigrants "often (have) superstitious, though not reverential, awe of the religious observances to which they are accustomed . . ."[35]

Writers such as the famed Jacob A. Riis, who in 1899 observed the worship of saints among immigrants from the village of Auletta, were astonished to see the lengths to which immigrants went in order to worship any of a number of deities.[36] Along with the worship of saints, there were the offsetting powers of evil invested in the working of those who had the evil eye.[37] As in southern Italy, saints were invoked to protect loved ones against the transgression of the evil eye. In fact, the role of saints in this regard was intensified in New Jersey and New York as, not surprisingly, Irish-American priests generally refused to intercede against the intrusions of the evil eye.[38] On those occasions when saints proved to be ineffectual, people turned to another rural custom—that of wearing protective amulets. for example, an account written in Rochester asserts that the:

24

best way of protecting yourself from the Devil was to carry a pointed amulet, preferably a horn, so that you could grasp it when someone with the evil eye looked at you. If you did not have the amulet, then the next best thing you could do was to form your hand in the shape of two horns.[39]

The same menacing evil emanating from the evil eye also emerged from the witches of New Jersey and News York. Disease and personal misfortunes were typically blamed on the workings of a "strega," or witch, a practice which did not die with the immigrant generation.[40] Witches were seen as sheer repositories of creative evil, people who devoted their lives to the acquisition and practice of terror. A "frattura," or the curse of a witch, was "far more deliberate and insidious than the evil eye, for it presupposed the services of a witch with a professional knowledge of black magic."[41] "Professional" was not a random choice of words. Some immigrants believed that witches received specialized training in the southern Italian town of Benevento.[42] The social worker Phyllis Williams writes that after the "witches received their instructions there they went around the villages seeking to do harm either because they had a grudge against someone or 'just for the devil of it'."[43] Wlliams' observation, though important, misses a key element in the perception of witches—their professional status in the eyes of many southern Italian immigrants. Witches earned a living through the collection of fees for their services, thereby receiving a grudging respect as independent practitioners. They were available to anyone who wanted to settle an old score—and were willing to pay money for that pleasure.[44]

What Their Religion Meant

Popular rituals instilled a semblance of personal control. We are thus confronted with religious rites which served as one of the few avenues of creative working class self-management. And there were other magical rituals beside those of saints and witches. Rituals conducted during the feast of St. John the Baptist at Manhattan Baxter Street Church and Hoboken's Santa Maria Church exemplify the use of rural theology to gain some personal control. These feasts, which took place annually on 24 June, featured attempts to glimpse at a young girl's future marriage. On the evening before the feast, Italian-American girls placed an egg in a glass of water. The following morning, sign readers interpreted the girl's future marriage through a consideration of the configuration of the water bubbles in the glass. Reportedly, this custom worked only during the time of the feast. Attempts to use it at other times were futile.[45]

Rituals such as this bring us to another aspect of Italian people's religion. While fear of the seemingly unmanageable world provided a central rationale for a theology of tactical defense, the pragmatic thrust of a theology designed to meet immediate needs also legitimized the social organizations within which workers lived. For instance, egg readings legitimized the maintenance of a known and accepted social universe. The outer boundaries of social reality, i.e., the limits binding one within an exploitative web of capitalist social relations, were already beyond the individual's capacity for immediate change. But the construction of institutions such as weddings were clearly within the province of the worker's control. Rituals such as egg reading reinforced this perception, and lent an air of optimism to an otherwise fatalistic culture.

There was even a discernible division of labor within the context of theological practice. Witches with various specialties and sign readers specializing in eggs served the function or normalizing a society administered by experts. Egg readers did not compete with witches, for they occupied different provinces. One learned within the ethnic enclave that the skilled had control over a specific portion of the social landscape. Just as in southern Italy, such rituals strengthened traditional ways of looking at the world. Initiative could be carried only so far. Rituals which exuded habitualization limited the range of possible human action. We are thus confronted with the spectacle of workers who often question a Roman Catholic Church that seemingly infringed upon conservative tradition.

With such perceptions paramount in the lives of Italian workers, a Catholic doctrine which emphasized an unworkable set of absolute Christian ethics appeared, at best, irrelevant. It was precisely those high-minded values that Irish-Catholicism stressed. One young Irish-American in the late 19th century recalled how he dreaded the frightening priest, whose Lenten sermons "scared me into a nervous misery although I was not in the least a sensitive child."[46] Irish Catholicism closely resembled the Protestantism of the 19th century in a doctrinal intolerance.[47] This attitude was rooted in the particular Catholicism of Ireland, where rituals such as the Mass were conducted with a reverence unheard of in rural Italy. It was most clearly embodied in a formal and unyielding theological system that lacked the fluidity and ethical relevance of Italian rural religion.[48] Represented in the very architecture of the Irish-American church, this system employed ornamentation which "represents the light of faith which the Dominicans carried in their combat with heresy."[49] Integral to Irish Catholicism was Irish nationalism, a nationalism which proudly featured Irish saints who were there to be revered rather than used as intermediaries in a harsh world. As Bossy suggests in *Christianity in the West,* some saints function as a "superior godparent, somebody you could talk to, as Joan of Arc did . . ."[50] This characterization does not apply to Irish saints, whose distance precludes friendship. Instead, St. John's Church in Newark featured statues of Irish saints who occupied "positions of honor (that) are wisely assigned to the great Patron and Patroness of the Irish race."[51]

The clear national pride of the Irish Church—which did little on that level alone to make the Italian-American feel comfortable—matched a theology of serious moral purpose on the local level. Differing little in intent or appearance from Anglo-American reform groups of the Progressive era, the "parochial societies" of the Irish-American Church worked to protest "profanity, blasphemy, and immorality." Holding demonstrations in Elizabeth, Paterson, and Jersey City, such groups as the Holy Name Society worked to impress upon immigrants the importance of accepting a Christianity replete with a moral zeal unknown in Italian churches. In Newark, Protestant officials lay aside doctrinal differences with Irish Catholics in order to pursue a Christianity that was morally absolute. For example, a description from 1907 reads:

> A few Protestant gentlemen took part in the procession in this city, including Police Justice David T. Howell. Individual members of the Holy Name Society have another duty to perform besides taking part in parades, approaching the Sacraments at stated times and refraining from blasphemy and profanity—when walking alone the highways and byways or employed at their daily labors, let them uncover their heads whenever they hear the Name of God taken in vain or the Holy Name blasphemed, raise their hearts to Heaven and say, "Blessed be the Name of God," or "Blessed be the Name of Jesus . . ."[52]

Irish Catholicism's moral purpose was undoubtedly bourgeois in its cultural implications. Confident moral zeal indicated a belief in the relevance of planning for a future which would be qualitively better than the present. To cite an obvious example, heaven was something in preparation for which to discipline oneself; an avoidance of "profanity, blasphemy, and immorality" constituted progress towards that end. It was a theological strategy of positive construction, one that differed dramatically from the defensive thrust of rural Italian theology. Irish Catholicism, like its Anglo-Protestant counterpart, was pragmatic only in order to serve higher moral purposes. The advice of Bishop Wigger of Newark that Irish Catholics utilize a specific method in order to avoid blasphemy illustrates how moral earnestness gave rise to seemingly pragmatic attitudes:

> Say to him that every time he swears or blasphemes let him fine himself—take ten cents out of one pocket, put it into another and give the money to the poor. Let him do this and he will soon break himself of the habit, for there is nothing which appeals to the heart and conscience of some men and tends to refresh the memory like touching the pocketbook.[53]

Pragmatism in Italian Catholicism had nothing to do with the moral absolutism advocated by Wigger and other officials of the American Catholic Church. Because this was a central religious difference with respect to both Irish Catholicism and Anglo-American Protestantism, it merits an elaboration.

The emphasis on a pragmatism devoid of higher ideals had its basis in the Hellenic conception of "pragmatikos." This pre-Christian idea of value had, as its foundation, the concern that something had worth because it worked in the social context of daily life. Such a vantage point did not easily lend itself to more abstract notions of good and evil. Workers consequently determined the worth of a religious belief by its apparent ability to produce desired ends. Italian rural theology thus "employed" and "fired" saints with dizzying regularity. The philosophical absolutes of Catholic doctrine became irrelevant in such a system. People could avoid evil and misfortune through any of a number of devices— anything went so long as it seemed to produce desired results. In the case of saints, we know that Italian peasants openly discarded holy relics when they did not do what they were supposed to do. This tradition continued in New Jersey and New York well into the 20th century. Thus, Rochester residents spoke of Italian-American workers who burst into church with the intention of destroying a saint's statue and replacing it with another which they hoped would fulfill the purpose assigned to it. This was evident in the New York metropolitan area as well through the 1940s. Such behavior horrified an Irish-American clergy steeped in a theology which emphasized piety and devotion to Christian ideals.

The conditional reverence exhibited towards saints, Jesus, and God was, from the perspective of Church officials, bad enough. Other aspects of Catholic life among the men, and the amount of money contributed to Catholic causes, further irritated Irish-American clergy. Julian Miranda, whose grandfather had emigrated from the Sicilian village of Castlebuono in 1907, recalls that southern "Italian men were not so church scrupulous as the women although they were Catholic." Another commentator remarks that "among Italians . . . religion was strictly for women, and, as in Italy, generally even those men considered devout absented themselves from services with a studied and uniform regularity."[54] Scholars have pointed to the preponderance of women in church devotions, while novelists such as Garibaldi M. Lapolla have focused on the primary importance of women in Italian-American religious rituals. That importance rested in a belief in the female's ability to be more readily understood by the saint to whom she prayed. Women embodied suffering, a suffering intensified by childbirth, thus making women physically akin to the powerful Madonna.[55]

As important as their similarity to the Madonna was the cultural centrality of women, who generally exercised control over the home in a way not apparent in the dominant American culture through the mid-20th century.[56] That power made them a logical emissary to the world of supernatural dieties, who were thought to respond most favorably to those who merit respect. Rural Italian society had long emphasized the dominant position of the wife and mother; they could not be replaced as easily as fathers and husbands. Devotion to the

Madonna, who, as a woman, soared above men in terms of everyday practical importance, expressed this central cultural motif.

Irish Catholicism did not emphasize a strict division between the religious importance of men and women. Nor did Anglo-American Protestantism. In both of these theological systems, men and women subscribed to a set of rigid moral standards in which the practicality of those standards was a secondary consideration in the pursuit of moral absolutes. The Italian religious system accorded women a primary role in devotional services precisely because the sole objective was to get practical results, and the cultural primacy of the female, along with her physical kinship with the Madonna, made her the logical choice. Practicality was never a route to spiritual fulfillment; it was always the end objective.

Italian theology thus embraced the world in a different way than did Irish Catholicism. Designed as a defensive strategy to cope with the status quo, it did not seek to move beyond in hopes of building a better world. Its religious ethics were eclectic at best, and they were always modified to meet the situation at hand. Its only coherent philosophy was one of immediacy and defense against a hostile world not subject to change. Italian Catholics did not exhibit the rational consistency of either Irish Catholicism or Anglo-American Protestantism, a consistency always synthesized in some kind of higher order exuding moral absolutes. They viewed reality as hostile, arbitrary, and irrational, and their defensive theological categories were designed accordingly.

Workers' theology became apparent in the elaborate public displays of Italian-American feasts, during which religious rituals expressed defensive strategies founded of fear. Guided by spontaneous behavior, these rituals lacked the rigid and temporally disciplined quality of Irish Catholic services, as Robert Orsi has suggested.[57] Any emphasis on a disciplined religious ritual equated with "worship" as such was relegated to an obscure position during the feast. Throughout, the concern was a public and unpremediated defense against the onslaught of misfortune.

Rather than seeking higher moral ideals through disciplined worship, participants in the feast achieved some semblance of safety in the world through devotion to caring saints and the purchase of charms. Devotion to saints often reached intense heights of self-inflicted pain. Thus, Riis wrote in 1899 that a "woman carries a mighty candle on her bare shoulder, walking barefoot on the hot asphalt." He went on. "Some march barefoot the six miles and over from Mulberry Street, choosing the roughest pavements and kneeling on the sharpest stones . . . lest there should be none sharp enough; the most devout carry flints in their pockets to put under their knees." This intensity did not wane with the immigrant generation. Thirty-six years later Lapolla observed that at the Feast of Saint Elena in Harlem:

29

dozens of . . . men and women both, would . . . get on their knees and cry aloud or mutter wild, incoherent prayers, bearing their breasts, raising their hands with fingers widespread.[58]

Workers carried statues of the saints to be worshipped in these processions. The faithful rushed out to pin money on the saint as another form of devotion.

Purchasing charms was the other public way of warding off danger for another year. Church members set up booths along the sidewalk, offering an assortment of horns, hunchbacks, and wax body parts, charms proudly displayed in the numerous parades which the feast featured.

Another important part of the feast was the enormous outlay of food present at every turn. Neighbors and visitors alike gathered for dinners that went on for hours. Snacks were offered continuously between meals and they could be found in both private homes and in booths on the street. Just as Riis had spoken of the "cry of the chestnut-vendor" and "pink lemonade . . . hawked along the curb." Lapolla later on tells us that the "sidewalks were lined with booths, each booth strung with dried nuts and laden with masses of tinted cakes and torroni."

All three aspects of the ceremony—devotions to the saints, charms, and food—attempted to ward off misfortune or, especially in the case of food, to affirm a momentary sense of personal safety. The threat of hunger was a lingering fear of both the immigrants and their descendants through the middle of the 20th century. Accordingly, an elaborate and abundant display of food symbolized a momentary harmony with the world in a vivid, physical sense. As the reformer Anna Ruddy wrote, Italian workers at *la festa della Madonna di Monte Carmine* noticed a "pale and pinched" child's face. A "feast of good things to eat that day" would alleviate the boy's hunger pangs temporarily.[59]

The need to ease anxieties intensified in an urban and industrialized environment. Italian-American workers clung to the festive abundance of food as a public symbol of temporary order and serenity. Festival booths attempted to convey the yearning for social rhythm and personal order—both strong emotional components of personal safety and security. The offering of traditional foodstuffs in large amounts underscored the cultural ideals of familiarity and consistency. Food booths at the feast managed to subdue temporarily one of the worker's greatest fears—impending hunger. This was a reassuring notion in a culture steeped in distrust and fear. "A feeling of security," dietary scholars tell us, "is associated with orderliness or a lack of anxiety and tension over whether food will be forthcoming. Certain foods foster (emotional) security more than others even apart from their ability to satisfy hunger."[60]

So again we find ourselves in an essentially defensive struggle. The individual worker has a self-image of powerlessness rooted in the reality of the worker's place in the social hierarchy of both rural Italy and New Jersey and New York. Italian religious rites helped to perpetuate this self-image. There was no place in this system for an individual to aspire to a higher moral plane through worship. The individual worker was effectively crushed by both the dominant American culture and the oppressive conservatism of Italian-American views of the world. No wonder then that the efforts of Italian religious reformers generally fell on deaf ears.

Evangelical Solutions

Italian Catholics displayed little interest in the idea of an independent path to salvation. Accordingly, Protestant reformers found few Italians ready for conversion. Nonetheless, Protestants made many attempts to attract Italian-Americans into the Protestant fold, culminating in the 1887 establishment of the Mt. Pleasant Baptist Church in Newark. In 1894 the Buffalo Baptist Union "turned towards the large growing settlements of Italians, with a deepening conviction that effort should be made to evangelize them." The first Italian Mission began in 1897, and another Brooklyn evangelical effort, the Ainslie Street Baptist Church, was established in 1900. Other areas of New Jersey and New York, among them Mt. Vernon, Troy, Albany, Rochester, and Passaic, saw organized and zealous efforts designed to draw Italians away from Catholicism.[61]

The most prominent of the Italian Protestant reformers was Angelo diDomenica. A prolific writer and pamphleteer, he authored such works as *Sieto Stato Battezzato?* (Have you been Baptized?); *Chi Sono I Pentecostoli?* (Who are the Pentecostals?); *America Is Good to Me; Is the Pope the Representative of Christ on Earth, or the Successor of Peter?;* and *Protestant Witness of a New American.* The son of poor peasants from the village of Schiavi d'Abruzzo, diDomenica first became acquainted with evangelical preachers through his older brother, who had been converted through the effort of an Italian preacher at the Five Points Mission House in Manhattan. In *Protestant Witness,* diDomenica recalls a life of gambling. He then explains how his brother's angry indictment had filled him with guilt and foreboding about his future. This culminated in his conversion.[62]

diDomenica did indeed turn his attention from gambling. He spent the next several years engaged in evangelical work. He held open-air services in Newark. He traveled to the North Orange Baptist Church in Orange, New Jersey to preach to Italian workers on Sundays. Finally he became involved in the Home Mission Society of Buffalo.

Despite diDomenica's unending optimism, the actual rate of conversion to Protestantism among Italian-Americans remained low. The absolute number of

Italian-American Protestants remained low in New Jersey and New York between the late 19th century and the middle of the 1930s, as the research of Silvano Tomasi reveals.[63] By 1917 the absolute numbers of Italian-American Protestants in the New Jersey/New York area had not risen dramatically. The Protestant theologian, Antonio Mangano, compiled statistics in 1917. They illustrate that no more than 1.8% of all Italian-Americans had been converted to Protestantism.[64] In two New York boroughs—Brooklyn and Queens—only 0.4% of all Italian-Americans were Protestant by 1935.[65]

Thus, the earlier optimism of a missionary such as diDomenica proved to be unfounded. Italian immigrants and their descendants did not turn to Protestantism, despite their differences with the Irish hierarchy of the Catholic Church. An examination of diDomenica's writings helps to explain why this was so. Like Irish Catholic spokesman Paul Flynn, diDomenica stresses the individual's responsibility for salvation. Salvation, as an absolute moral ideal, was itself a problem within the Italian theological sphere. That issue aside, diDomenica's conversion experience was highly personal, centered in the control of the soul. In diDomenica's accounts, little distinguishes the self-discipline which allegedly adds up to material wealth from salvation attained through prayer. Both goals placed at the forefront the qualities of thrift and industry.

However, diDomenica failed to comprehend that he was advocating another form of the dominant culture's conception of social mobility—a conception already being redefined within the context of working class life. Replacing material poverty with spiritual poverty, diDomenica proposed that the latter resulted from "popery." Empty rituals, poor church attendance, and the outlay of scarce resources on feasts all added up to the presence of a "laziness" and "lack of thrift" which yielded spiritual poverty. diDomenica worked his way "up" from employment as a laborer in a shoe factory—and thereby entered into God's graces—only when he had shunned the "moral and spiritual condition of the Italian people" in a highly personal way.

Thus, the Protestant road to moral purity was a lonely one. According to Italian-American workers, Protestantism lacked the comforting reassurances yearned for in an essentially hostile world. Commenting on Presbyterian missionaries in 1918, Enrico C. Sartorio noted that there was a "chasm between the mentality of simple Italian women and that of the American lady parish visitor . . . (who enforces her) views without much consideration for the views and traditions of the other race."[66] Alberto Pecorini, whose observations of Italian-American laborers are recorded in numerous essays, said that Protestants "did not make proselytes among Italian immigrants, as they might have expected to do in the case of other races since Italians lacked that individual evolved conscience that Protestantism presupposes."[67] Pecorini understood that the

Protestant way to salvation, like the Irish Catholic way, presumed the Christian's adherence to an individualistic creed. That creed never figured centrally in rural Italian culture at large—not to mention its religious component. Accordingly, even if one assumed there was a road to salvation, it was necessarily a group road, one on which like-minded workers comforted each other along the way.

Numerous workers commented that Protestantism's emphasis on the lone individual was not soothing in the same way as a group's relationship with a saint.[68] Nor did the whole enterprise of striving for salvation, a process inherently optimistic, fit in with the defensive thrust of Italian theology. Italian-American conceptions of God always emphasized the notion of fate. "I always offer all my suffering to God: May it be his will," one female worker wrote to the Madonna in 1947.[69] Such a perspective did not induce a turn towards an individual initiative designed to achieve pure goodness.

Indeed, the idea of human perfectability was not accepted. Italian theology through the first half of the 20th century typically remained an arena in which bargains with powerful saints were struck, saints who could hopefully provide protection against misfortune. Optimistic individualism could never transcend the assumption of fate.

Conclusion

"Culture has continuity," Jacques Barzun once wrote. Antonio Gramsci suggested the same perspective throughout many of his writings. For Italian peasants in Italy and Italian-American workers in New Jersey and New York, the essence of their theological continuity lay in the absence of a notion of progress itself. As scholars such as Ninian Smart, Nancey Murphy and, to a lesser extent, Andrew Louth have all suggested, the concept of progress in Christianity is generally inseparable from broader patterns of Western thought over the last several centuries.[70] Thus, modern theology, like its ideological cousins, has held out the belief that the world is capable of being transformed for the better. Indeed, modern Christianity has typically institutionalized such hopes. It became common to assume that such optimism could transform human beings and the societies they inhabit.

But such social gospels could never take root in Italian Catholicism. That theology was part of a total cultural context with its own intergenerational rhythms. A perceived stream of experience united the generations, maintained by exploitative social conditions in both rural Italy and industrial, urban America. Italian popular religion thus presented a reality at least partially shaped—and explained—by subjective perceptions of ultimate questions not answerable by the main currents of Christian thought.

Official Catholic doctrines were simply not functional within the context of Italian rural experience. Needless to say, such doctrines were not always functional within urban Italian-American life either. The resources of grace in Catholic and Protestant doctrines could not find meaning in the social spheres inhabited by peasants or urban workers. Meanings cannot be projected; they must be inflated by the air of lived experience.

Different experiences producing different religious systems sensitize us to the fact that there were very different cultural spheres within both Italy and the United States. In addition, there were various religious spaces within Catholicism itself. As we have seen, there was a persistent tension between these categories. In any event, the religion of defensive struggle evident among rural Italian folk continued among their heirs in New Jersey and New York. As I have tried to show, this religion continued well into the middle of the 20th century and possibly beyond, pushed onward by a capitalist system that tended to perpetuate the same habits of emotional subordination which had once been the seemingly intractable quality of feudalism in the Italian countryside.

Notes

1. The most persuasive evidence to date is Colleen Johnson's *Growing Up and Growing Old in Italian-American Families,* New Brunswick, NJ, Rutgers University Press 1985. She points out that "over time; the socialization processes are colored by the character of the social network." She adds that where "the social network is connected by relatives who share the same views and who are in frequent interaction with each other, it is proposed that the potential for change is minimized" (p. 13).
2. The "She-Wolf," in *The She-Wolf and Other Stories*, Berkeley, CA, University of California Press 1962, p. 3. Relevant secondary accounts recently published include Barbara C. Pope, "The origins of southern Italian Good Friday processions," in Paola A. Sensi and Anthony Julian Tamburri, eds., *Italian Americans Celebrate Life: The Arts and Popular Culture*, West Lafayette, IN, Purdue University Press 1990, pp. 155–68; and Gabriele Monaco, *La Madonna di Trapani; storia, culto, folklore*, Naples, Laurenziana 1981
3. Villari, *Italian Life in Town and Country*, New York, NY, G. P. Putnam's Sons 1902.
4. For a discussion of church lands in this regard, consult Leonard Covello's *The Social Background of the Italian-American School Child*, Totowa, NJ, Rowman and Littlefield 1972, pp. 136–40. Also see Martin Clark's *Modern Italy*, New York, NY, Longman 1990; and Giovanni Monfroni, *Societae mercato della terra: la vendita dei terreni della Chiesa in Campania dopo l'unita*, Naples, Guida 1983.
5. In this regard, the peasants interviewed by Richard Bagot in *The Italians of Today*, Chicago, IL, Mills and Boon 1913, were characterized as cynical, also refer to Watson, *Roman Private Law Around 200 B.C.,* Edinburgh, Edinburgh University Press 1971, p. 90.
6. Covello, "The Church as an economic and educational force," in *The Social Background of the Italo-American School Child*, p. 137.
7. Dennis M. Smith, *Italy: A Modern History*, Ann Arbor, MI, University of Michigan Press 1959, p. 87.
8. See Leopoldo Franchetti, *La Sicilia nel 1876: condizioni Politiche E Amministrative*, Firenze, Vallecchi 1925; and Sidney Sonnino's *La Sicilia nel 1876: I Contadini*, Firenze, Vallecchi 1925.
9. Covello, "The role of the priest," in *The Social Background of the Italo-American School Child*, pp. 137–9.
10. Ibid.

11. In Covello, *The Social Background of the Italo-American School Child*, p. 139.
12. Flynn, *History of St. John's Church, Newark*, Newark, NJ, Press of the New Jersey Trade Review 1908.
13. Bossy, *Christianity in the West, 1400–1700*, New York, NY, Oxford University Press 1985, pp. 3–13.
14. Edward Wakin, *Enter the Irish-American*, New York, NY, Cromwell 1976, p. 86. Also refer to Silvano Tomasi's *Piety and Power*, New York, NY, Center for Migration Studies 1975; Leonard Bacigalupo, "Some religious aspects involving the interaction of the Italians and the Irish," in *Italians and Irish in America*, Francis Femminella, ed. New York, NY, American Italian Historical Association 1985, pp. 115–29; Carmine A. Loffredo, A history of the Roman Catholic school system in the Archdiocese of Newark, New Jersey, 1900–1965, Ed.D. dissertation, Rutgers University 1967; and Dennis J. Starr's "Roman Catholic Church" in *The Italians of New Jersey: A Historical Introduction and Bibliography*, Newark, NJ, New Jersey Historical Commission 1985, p. 36.
15. In Jerre Mangione's *Mount Allegro*, New York, NY, Columbia University Press 1981, p. 68.
16. W. H. Agnew, "Pastoral care of Italian children in America: some plain facts about the condition of our Italian children," *Ecclesiastical Review* (March 1913), p. 258.
17. Quoted in Tomasi, "American views of Italian newcomers," *Piety and Power*, p. 45.
18. Flynn, "First Italian mission in Newark," in *History of St. John's Church, Newark*, p. 217.
19. Ibid., p. 216.
20. See Covello, "Cultural dissimilarity of Italian contadino as a basis for conflict in the United States," *The Social Background of the Italo-American School Child*, p. 278. Also refer to the *Souvenir History of Transfiguration Parish—Mott Street, New York, 1827–1897*, New York, NY, privately published 1897, p. 278.
21. Anastasi, *The History of the Church of St. Anthony of Padua, Hackensack*, New Jersey, n.p., 1962.
22. Ibid., p. 5.
23. Ibid.
24. Ibid., pp. 5–6.
25. Ibid., p. 12.
26. See Loffredo's discussion of Our Lady of Mount Carmel Church in Newark, in "A history of The Roman Catholic school system in the Archdiocese of Newark, New Jersey, 1900–1965," pp. 100–1.
27. Quoted in Tomasi's *Piety and Power*, p. 95.
28. Ibid., pp. 177–85.
29. Quoted in E. E. Chivers, "Our Baptist Italian mission work," *The Baptist Home Mission Monthly* (May 1905), p. 198.
30. Loffredo, "A history of the Roman Catholic school system in the Archdiocese of Newark, New Jersey, 1900–1965," p. 101.
31. For example, see Bishop Wigger's views on the southern Italian practice of confirming infants. A succinct summary is found in Loffredo, "A history of the Roman Catholic school system in the Archdiocese of Newark, New Jersey, 1900–1965," p. 323.
32. Refer to "L'attivita religiosa della italiani in America," *L'Opinione* (29 March 1906), p. 1.
33. Quoted in Tomasi, *Piety and Power*, p. 161.
34. For example, see Viola Roseboro, "The Italians of New York," *Cosmopolitan* (January 1888), especially p. 405.
35. Roseboro, "The Italians of New York," p. 405.
36. Riis, "Feast-days in Little Italy," *Century Magazine* (August 1899), p. 491.
37. Two literary depictions of this belief are found in Mangione, *Mount Allegro*, pp. 100–8; and Pietro di Donato's *Three Circles of Light*, New York, NY, Messner 1960, pp. 157–60. Also refer to Edward S. Gifford, *The Evil Eye*, New York, NY, Macmillian 1958; and Phyllis Williams, *South Italian Folkways in Europe and America*, New Haven, CT, Yale University Press 1938, pp. 141–5.
38. As Riis pointed out in "Feast days in Little Italy," the protecting saint belonged to the workers and not to the Church hierarchy.

39. Mangione, *Mount Allegro*, p. 104.
40. For example, Jerry Della Femina speaks of seeing this as a young boy in the 1950s. See *An Italian Grows in Brooklyn*, Boston MA, Little, Brown 1978, pp. 75–6.
41. Mangione, *An Italian Grows in Brooklyn*, p. 104.
42. See Williams, *South Italian Folkways in Europe and America*, p. 144.
43. Ibid.
44. See Mangione's discussion of Rosina, pp. 104–7.
45. Consult two newspaper articles devoted to this ritual—in the *New York Times*, 13 June 1913, p. 30; and the *Corriere della Sera* 24 June 1909, n.p.
46. Quoted in Wakin, *Enter the Irish-American*, pp. 97–8.
47. For instance, see the remarks of Father Thomas J. McCluskey in Flynn, *History of St. John's Church, Newark*, p. 101.
48. See the position taken by Bishop O'Connor in Flynn, *History of St. John's Church*, p. 14.
49. Ibid., p. 19.
50. Bossy, *Christianity in the West*, 1400–1700, p. 12.
51. Flynn, *History of St. John's Church, Newark*, pp. 19–20.
52. Ibid., p. 79.
53. Ibid., p. 81.
54. See Carl D. Hinrichsen, the history of the diocese of Newark, 1873–1901, Ph.D. dissertation, Catholic University of America 1962, pp. 317–18. Also refer to the oral interview of Julian Miranda in *The Immigrants Speak: Italian Americans Tell Their Story*, New York, NY, Center for Migration Studies 1979, pp. 131–2.
55. We see this portrayal in Michael DeCapite's Maria, New York, NY, John Day company 1943. Also see Lapolla's *The Grand Gennaro*, New York, NY, Vanguard Press 1935; and Robert Orsi's *The Madonna of 155th Street*, New Haven, CT, Yale University Press 1985.
56. For a persuasive argument about women who were central matriarchal figures, see Donna R. Gabbacia's *From Sicily to Elizabeth Street*, Albany, NY, State University of New York Press 1984.
57. Orsi, *The Madonna of 155th Street*, p. 2.
58. *The Grand Gennaro*, p. 46.
59. Ruddy, *The Heart of the Stranger*, New York, NY, Revell 1908, p. 69.
60. Miriam E. Lowenberg *et al.*, *Food and Man*, 2nd Ed, New York, NY, Wiley 1974, p. 147.
61. See the Summary of Chivers, "Our Baptist Italian mission work'.
62. *Protestant Witness of a New American*, Chicago, IL, The Judson Press 1956, pp. 26–7.
63. Tomasi, *Piety and Power*, pp. 155–8.
64. *Sons of Italy: A Social and Religious Study of the Italians in America*, New York, NY, Missionary Education Movement of the United States and Canada 1917.
65. Tomasi, *Piety and Power*, p. 158.
66. *Social and Religious Life of Italians in America*, Boston, MA, Christopher Publishing House 1918, p. 123.
67. Quoted in Alberto Giovannetti, *The Italians of America*, New York, NY, Manor Books 1979, p. 270.
68. An interesting summary of these views is found in May C. Marsh, The Life and work of the churches in an interstitial area, Ph.D. dissertation, New York University 1932.
69. Quoted in Orsi, *The Madonna of 155th Street*, p. 227.
70. Ninian Smart, *The Phenomenon of Christianity*, London, Collins 1979; Nancey Murphy, *Theology in the Age of Scientific Reasoning*, Ithaca, NY, Cornell University Press 1990; and Andrew Louth, *Discerning the Mystery*, Oxford, Clarendon Press 1983.

Study Questions

1. Write the citation for this article in correct AHA/Chicago form:

   _____

   _____

   _____

   _____

2. In your own words, write a one-sentence summary of the main point of this article:

   _____

   _____

   _____

   _____

3. List several reasons why this article is scholarly, rather than popular:

   _____

   _____

   _____

4. List five sources used in the compilation of this article:

   _____

   _____

5. Imagine that you have used this article as one of the entries for your annotated bibliography. Write a brief evaluative comment about this article.

   _____

   _____

   _____

Miss Erin: Nationalism, Feminism, and the Popular 19th Century Anglo-Irish Novel

Janet Madden

When we think of Anglo-Irish literature, two things come immediately to mind. One is the difficulty of definition, for, as its unwieldy name suggests, Anglo-Irish literature is a politically-charged hybrid, an English-language but Irish subject-centred body of writing which was initiated by Maria Edgeworth's *Castle Rackrent* (1800), and which was consolidated into a vital new national literature almost single-handedly by William Butler Yeats at the end of the 19th century. Our second perception is of a glorious (and sonorous) litany which stretches from Yeats, Synge, Joyce, Beckett, Moore, O'Connor, O'Flaherty and O'Faolain to those identified as the inheritors of that tradition—Higgins, Banville and Heaney. But this perceived notion of Anglo-Irish literature—what Frank O'Connor has called a "peculiarly masculine affair" (O'Connor 202)—does not merely reflect the sexism and elitism which have underpinned the image-crafting of Anglo-Irish literature. In its consciously hierarchical documentation, Anglo-Irish literary criticism has presented us with a resultant body of literature which reflects the consistent practice of literary apartheid, the systematic exclusion of writers who have not been judged worthy of receipt of the man-made mantle of literary/cultural approbation. Thus, in a cultural milieu which celebrates the masculine experience and dismisses the feminine as inconsequential, we should not be surprised to learn that of the hundreds of women who have written works which are by cultural definition Anglo-Irish, only the writings of a handful—Edgeworth, Somerville and Ross, Elizabeth Bowen, Mary Lavin, Kate O'Brien—have been deemed admissable to the canon. And, while Anglo-Irish literary criticism has begun, very slowly, to widen the parameters of its focus, especially in relation to the explosion of contemporary writing by women, it has ignored almost absolutely the existence of the phenomenally large output of a great number of female Anglo-Irish writers who, between the years 1875–1925, produced hundreds of Anglo-Irish novels. In the Irish Revival climate of political and cultural standard-bearing in response to the English hegemony, rejection of selected works is understandable. But, the wholesale policy of precluding any works which, on the basis of sales figures or target audience, might be tarred with the brush of "circulationist fiction" (Boyd 374) has resulted in a lop-sided tradition which, ironically, has been robbed of a great deal of energy. Writers who were most popular and most widely read in their lifetimes are now quite unknown, in spite of the wealth of information which they can give us about the taste of the reading public, the concerns of the community of Anglo-Irish writers, and, indeed, the backdrop against which the works of Yeats, Synge or Joyce—or, for that matter, Somerville and Ross—are held up as paradigms. The "popular" Anglo-Irish writers provide the connective tissue for the tradition; an analysis of their work also provides some unexpected insights into the real issues at work in Irish society.

One such illuminating work is *Miss Erin* (1898), which clearly shows not only why its author, M. E. Francis, was one of the most widely read of 19th century Anglo-Irish writers, but which also reveals the subcutaneous writer-reader identification which is particularly and subterraneously female. *Miss Erin* is, first, a female *bildungsroman* with which the reader can immediately sympathize. But Francis' true inspiration comes with her carefully-detailed use of the morphology of the fairy tale, which she infuses with the political implications of Erin's deliciously tempestuous love affair with an English politician. The result is a fantasy of feminine triumph—albeit with a peculiar twist of Irish nationalism.

Francis uses the Anglo-Irish literary tradition of "sentimental patriotism" (Flanagan 36) in order to establish the novel's comic disparity of vision, and her tongue-in-cheek exposure of Erin's intense but naive patriotism is always carried out in specifically feminine terms. Thus, the extremely serious issue of Erin's committment to the cause of Irish freedom is played out in a scene in which Erin is persuaded to attend a fancy-dress ball. Having rejected her friend's suggestion that she wear "a green dress all over shamrocks and carry a green flag in one hand and a harp in the other" (Francis 145), Erin determines to portray a Connemara peasant girl. But in her short blue dress and red cloak, she is mistaken for Little Red Riding Hood.

To Erin's intense chagrin, she does indeed succeed in representing *"something* Irish" (Francis 160): in her satin dress and velvet cloak which have been made by a French *modiste,* she is the visible symbol of a self-deception which comes perilously close to the burlesquing of the Irish nationalist beliefs which she so fervently espouses. On the morning after the disastrous ball, she is filled with loathing at the self-indulgence which has led her into the misrepresentation of all that is most important to her. Already coming to a realisation of the way in which she has travestied herself, she is "very kindly" warned that

> . . . everything unites to trammel you. Youth, wealth, luxurious surroundings, the love of your friends, all will hem you in. This will be your tragedy. You will struggle and long to do something wonderful and heroic—and you will be obliged to content yourself with a happy girl's life (Francis 169).

The unerring clarity of this analysis points to the crux of Erin's revolutionary struggle, for, as Francis is writing for a female audience, she must provide Erin with the potential for being "trammeled." As a turn-of-the-century popular novelist, the only possible complication with which she can endow her heroine comes in relation to love.

Miss Erin is a novel of many levels: as well as a study of the psychology of patriotism, it is also a rather sophisticated examination of the effects of emotional deprivation. For Erin, these are twin difficulties: her mythic vision of herself as an Irish patriot is in some part conceived as a compensatory alternative to her orphanhood and her confused sense of self-identity, which Francis suggests is a specifically female state and which she emphasises through embedded references to fairy tales. This method of suggesting universality finds reinforcement through Francis' creation of a tragic vision to offset the comic. The tension between the two modes informs both the construction of the novel and Erin's maturation process; during the course of her growth from girl to woman, Erin alternates between such comic expressions of selfhood as the fancy-dress ball scene and heartfelt alliance with forces which would consume her. Over and over Francis anticipates Patrick Pearse's 1915 drama *The Singer* and articulates its theme of blood-sacrifice. Erin not only belives that there could be no more glorious fate than to die in setting Ireland free. She also expresses her emotional attraction to both civil disobedience and the tragic consequences of enacted beliefs: her favourite story is *The Antigone* because "it was grand of her to lay down her life for a sacred cause" (Francis 125).

From the first, as befits a novel which derives from the fairy tale tradition, Erin's life is unusual, even improbable. Ireland's importance to the novel lies in its embodiment of the exotic, and Francis establishes Ireland as the only milieu for the formation of Erin's character; as the place of tragic history and passionate emotion, it stands in contrast to the rational and civilised settings of England and Belgium. The Ireland of the Irish peasantry, in which Erin spends her early childhood, is an otherworld which the English cannot understand, or even imagine. And when Erin is forced to leave Ireland at the age of thirteen— an age which quintessentially embodies the adolescent condition, she clings to the Irish identity which her name expresses and which bespeaks both her tribal identification with the peasantry and the weight of the past which simultaneously sustains and oppresses both Erin and her country.

From the novel's opening scenes, in which Erin is presented as an archetypal female foundling, and in which her dying father "dedicates" and "consecrates" his child as "the last proof of her father's love for his country and hers" (Francis 33), Erin is catapulted into a series of households in widely varying places and circumstances. In each of these successive foster homes, Erin enacts the roles of the helpless female child; Francis reiterates the words "impotent" and "impotence" in order to stress Erin's powerlessness, which, appropriately for a female child, increses as she grows older. Her dependence on strangers for every kind of

41

sustenence begins with an Irish peasant wet-nurse who not only literally ensures Erin's survival, but who also comes to stand as a prototypical mother-figure. And time with this incarnation of mother-Ireland imprints on Erin the reality of the lives which provide the rhetoric for nationalist idealism. The loss of this first and most elemental foster-family, and, in particular, her foster-mother, radicalises Erin, and leads her directly to the renewal of the vows made on her behalf by her father. But Erin's own vows are made in specific terms of feminine sensibility. Deprived of her human mother for the second time, Erin turns to "mother-Ireland." In her grief, she stretches herself on her favourite hillside and feels "soothed and comforted" in the belief that she is "lying on her mother's bosom" (Francis 105). This alliance with female space expresses physically Erin's later explanation of the nurturance which the land gives her, and how, in consequence, she has loved and lived for it ever since" (Francis 181).

In *The Triumph of Prudence Over Passion* (1781), a novel written by "an Irish lady," the heroine declares

> I see no reason why women should not be patriots; for surely, if tyranny and oppression are established in a country they are more liable to suffer from it, both in their persons and property than men . . . (232)

and thus, even before the officially sanctioned inception of Anglo-Irish literature as a distinctive body of writing, establishes an analogy between the subjection of Ireland to England and the subjection of women to men. This theme runs steadily through Anglo-Irish literature written by women, and although for Erin, such economic feminism never becomes a personal issue, she does earmark her inherited fortune for use in the alleviation of the general conditions of the peasantry. Erin's indirect contribution to the lives of women—another turn of the plot which is attributable to Francis' employment of fairy-tale touches—is, however, directly allied to her own deeply frustrated desire to obtain control over her own affairs.

As Francis constantly reminds the reader, the deeply frustrating condition of being female is fundamental to every nuance of the plot of *Miss Erin*. Erin is educated only because her uncle thinks that "it would be great fun to make a blue-stocking of her" (Francis 67). When Erin's first poem is accepted for publication in *The Nation,* she is cheered as "the patriot's daughter," rather than as a poet in her own right. And, to her dismay, instead of receiving praise for her espousal of the nationalist cause, she is informed that "the cause'll get on without ye . . . it's men's work . . . Pray for the cause as much as you like and do what ye can for the poor" (Francis 112). Finally, in a fittingly ironic feminine equivalent of her father's sentence of transportation, Erin is "shipped off" to an English girls' school in Brussels. Being sent to such a place, in such company, represents Erin's own Van Dieman's Land.

The sea journey to Brussels more than marks out Erin as an exile. It stands also as a metaphor for the journey to maturity on which she has unwillingly embarked. And, in her transition from child to woman, she appropriately has her first encounter with a young man who Francis clearly marks as Erin's adversary as well as her romantic interest. Erin's other relationship is formed on arrival at school, where she acquires her first friend, the daughter of an English aristocrat whose greatest concerns are putting up her hair, being laced into ball dresses and conducting pleasant rounds of visiting and shopping. Francis' novelistic attitudes are matched by Erin, who resists the alluring, yet constricting images with which her friend passes the time—Erin believes that she "has other things to do with my life" (Francis 141).

Most of Erin's plans, of course, involve her schemes for the amelioration of the sufferings of the Irish peasantry, and for some time she does not understand the significance of her inheritance of her uncle's fortune; until her friend explains to her that she is "a landlord . . . actually one of those dreadful beings you used to hate so much" (Francis 142), Erin does not fully appreciate that she is hemmed in not only by gender and age, but also by the tentacles of patriarchial and imperialist power which control and administer her fortune for her. The ironies of Erin's rags-to-riches are complicated further by the reappearance of the young man of the sea voyage, for now begins Erin's most severe testing-time in which she must confront the most beguiling fantasy of the fairy tale—the transforming power of love.

From the beginning of this most complicated of courtships, Erins feels herself both "disenchanted" by the political views of her love-object and "oddly humiliated by him" (Francis 163). His determined egoism and cultural and gender sectionalism find expression in his "constitutional dislike for talking politics to women"; he informs Erin that

> Your lips were formed for quite a different prattle and your mind was meant to feed
> on other stuff—to me there is something so incongruous between yourself and your
> views that I feel personally affronted when I hear you discuss them (Francis 179).

His view of women as children is directly analogous to his perception of Ireland as a recalcitrant female child:

> We refused to put a knife into the hands of a child who is not to be trusted with
> it . . . I don't think you quite realise all that we have done for Ireland; we will do
> more yet if Ireland will only behave herself . . . (Francis 200).

The paternalistic tone of the "we" voice is met by Erin's determination to exercise her power over him, and, moreover, to enlist his help for her cause. Blinded by her own chauvinism, Erin therefore underestimates his. Both believe that "love can work a revolution in people's lives" (Francis 210); the irony of Francis' comic vision lies in each party's belief that the other will capitulate. Only gradually does Erin come to realise that "all this talk of love, and the power of love, and the changes which it might effect were meant to apply to her" (Francis 220).

A novelist less committed to the explorations of power and dominance would allow the novel to become a gentle comedy of errors which would lead to the exchange of politics for love and marriage. Francis, however, provides Erin with sufficient integrity to refuse marriage on terms which would leave her dependent on husbandly goodwill and permissions. Just as her lover feels that he cannot betray the trust which his political party has invested in him, so Erin counters his concept of masculine honour with her personal code of ethics—and, as wave-like movements of the plot develop and sustain the tension of principles versus love, Francis allows her heroine to achieve independence for the first time. Only in returning to Ireland as a mature woman, on her own terms, free at last of the "incubus" which she must "exorcise" (Francis 232) can Erin come to terms, too, with her childhood dreams of dramatic patriotism and her adult dreams of a marriage which will be a partnership of equals. In proving to her lover as well as to herself that "women could have principles as well as men, that they could be as steadfast, as determined" (Francis 220), Erin is transformed at a stroke from victim to role-model. With her economic independence, her realistic plans for the improvement of the Irish political situation, and a husband who has been converted to her views and who will work with her to achieve her aims, Erin is amply rewarded for her judicious exchange of her vision of sacrificial offering for fairy tale success. And, in modelling the behaviour and the possible chances of success for young, inexperienced, and even sometimes mistaken young women, M. E. Francis holds out to her audience the possibility of contracting a marriage in terms of mutual, as well as self, respect. The seriousness with which Francis handles her themes reveals her to be a writer who can do more than turn out a cliff-hanging plot and shrewdly gauge popular taste. With *Miss Erin,* Francis proves triumphantly that popular novels can be none the less intensely feminist for being feminine. And, like other writers of popular Anglo-Irish novels, Francis allows us a view of the world which may deflate some of our preconceptions about the value of popular fiction.

Works Cited

Boyd, Ernest M. *Ireland's Literary Renaissance.* New York: Alfred Knopf, 1922.

"By the Authoress of Emeline," *The Triumph of Prudence Over Passion; or, The History of Miss Mortimer and Miss Fitzgerald.* Dublin: Colbert, 1781.

Flanagan, Thomas. *The Irish Novelists 1800–1850.* New York: Columbia University Press, 1959.

Francis, M. E. *Miss Erin.* New York: Benziger, 1898.

O'Connor, Frank. *The Lonely Voice.* London: Macmillan, 1963

Sample Annotated Bibliographies

The student samples provide models to which you may refer as you compile your annotated bibliography project. They are not intended as models which you should follow exactly. Rather, they show how undergraduate students in two disciplines—English and History—have responded to the annotated bibliography assignment. In each case, the entries appear as they did in the original project.

These student samples provide models to which you should refer as you compile you own annotated bibliography project. They show how two El Camino College students in freshman-level English and History classes responded to their annotated bibliography assignments.

Note that the Annotated Bibliography project written for an English course utilizes the MLA citation form, while the Annotated Bibliography project written for a History course utilizes the AHA/Chicago citation form.

Student Sample Annotated Bibliography: English

Annotated Bibliography Project Cover Sheet

Project Title: <u>An Annotated Bibliography of Octavia E. Butler's *Kindred*</u>

Course: <u>English 1A</u>

Name: <u>Christina Rossi</u>

Date: <u>April 12, 1995</u>

Foster, Frances Smith. "Octavia Butler's Black Female Future Fiction." *Extrapolation* 23.1 (1982): 37–49.

In this article, Frances Smith Foster discusses Octavia Butler's use of black female characters in her futuristic science fiction novels. According to Foster, Butler is not just an average science fiction writer because she also incorporates racial and sexual issues into her stories. To illustrate how Butler achieves this aim, Foster examines three of her novels, *Patternmaster, Mind of My Mind,* and *Survivor,* which all deal with common themes. The story that the three novels tell takes place in a futuristic society where a virus spread by returning astronauts kills half of the world's population and causes mutations among children whose parents were afflicted with the disease. A heirarchy is developed within this society in which people with telepathic powers and great mental abilities are in control over the rest of the population. Foster points out that Butler's characters are equal, regardless of race or sex. Unlike many other authors, her main characters are strong, independent, black women.

By describing the main characters of the three novels, Foster demonstrates how the women evolve from positive characters to the heroines of the story (42). She contributes to the story by teaching a younger brother to defeat his older brother. In *Mind of My Mind,* the main female character is Mary, who "emerges as the protagonist," taking a greater part in the story than Amber does in *Patternmaster* (42). However, Mary still shares the focus of the novel with a man, her father, who has just as much power as she does. In *Survivor,* Foster reveals that the focus of the story is Alanna, who is the "heroine" of the novel (42). Unlike the two other main female characters, Alanna does not have powers of any kind and is said to be the "archetype" of a futuristic woman (42). Foster points out that all of Butler's main characters are black women and recognizes that Butler writes of black women because she is a black woman herself.

In writing this article, Foster clearly explains Octavia Butler's style of writing. She makes the point that people are equal in power, intelligence, and independence whatever their race or sex may be, which is useful in understanding Butler's writing. Foster further describes how Butler does focus on using black women as her main lead characters, unlike many contemporary science fiction authors, and argues this focus shows the importance and uniqueness of Butler's writing. She states that the main reason Butler uses black female characters is that she uses her own "experiences and sensitivities," which is both interesting and informative in that it offers an insight into the author's background and inspiration for her writing (42).

Govan, Sandra Y. "Connections, Links, and Extended Networks: Patterns In Octavia Butler's Science Fiction." *Black American Literature Forum* 18.2 (1984): 82–87.

In this work, Sandra Y. Govan demonstrates the connections, links, and extended networks of patterns in Octavia Butler's science fiction novels. Govan explains that Butler writes her novels in a connecting pattern by giving her characters similiar roles. She analyzes five of Butler's science fiction novels: *Patternmaster, Mind of My Mind, Survivor, Wild Seed,* and *Kindred.* In each example, Govan gives specific details of how Butler's characters all have equal power, whatever their sex or race may be. In writing this article, Govan describes the equal power of the many characters in Butler's novels in which "the struggle for power revolves around conflicts of will and the tests of survival a heroine endures" (83). When reading the novels, one will see "new links, new connections, and new variations in the patterns" of Butler's writing (87).

The prequel, *Wild Seed,* is about two immortals with different powers and goals. A man, Doro, who can sense people who have psychic gifts, wants a woman, Anyanwu, who can heal and alter her body into another form. In *Patternmaster,* Amber is a part of Anyanwu's family. She is an independent woman with healing powers and she teaches a younger brother to defeat his older brother. In *Mind of My Mind,* Mary is a direct part of Anyanwu's family, Doro's daughter. Mary is a fighter and a survivor with powers. Like Anyanwu, Mary has something Doro wants, though she realizes she cannot let him take over her life and so she proceeds to destroy him. Alanna plays the role of a "heroine" in the novel *Survivor* (85). With no powers, her strength "can be measured by her determination to live" (85). The novel *Kindred* is more an extended network than a connection, though there may be a connection between Dana and the other women in the past novels. Like Butler's other characters, Dana has "survival skills, and her determination to live is tested constantly" (86). Govan states that all of Octavia Butler's heroines are "strong protagonists, paired with, or matched against, an equally powerful male" (84).

Govan has written an article with value dealing with five of Octavia Butler's science fiction novels. Her specific examples from each novel explain to the reader how Butler changes science fiction by using a heroine, as opposed to a traditional male hero. Govan's connection of the patterns of Butler's novels helps the reader to understand how the novels all relate. The article is clearly focused and is an excellent source for learning more about Octavia Butler's science fiction novels. The only distracting aspect of this article is that Govan uses too many sources. This gets confusing at times, because it can be difficult to completely understand the claims that Govan makes without getting lost in the specific details of five different novels.

Govan, Sandra Y. "Homage to Tradition: Octavia Butler Renovates the Historical Novel." *Melus* 13. 1-2 (1986): 79–96.

In this article, Sandra Y. Govan examines how Octavia Butler uses the traditional historical novel as a base, and then, by incorporating slave naratives and science fiction, she renovates that form. As stated by Govan, Butler is an artistic and accomplished writer "conscious of the power of art to affect social perceptions and behaviors" (79). Butler uses her talent to teach important historical, racial, and sexual lessons without the reader being aware that learning is occurring. Explaining what makes up a slave narrative and how the slave narrative is related to the historical novel, Govan demonstrates what a good slave narrative consists of and what effects slave narratives have on people and society. Govan explains that Butler combines the historical novel, the slave narrative, and science fiction all into one new unique type of novel, and, in doing so, she is reaching a much broader audience that includes readers of all three styles of writing. Using two of Butler's novels, *Wild Seed* and *Kindred,* Govan shows the connection where the "historical novel, the slave narrative, and science fiction meet" (82). Both of the novels share three common points: the use of "black and white characters who move through an historically viable setting, the linkage through phenomenal psychic energy, and the emphasis on blood ties" (84).

The novel *Wild Seed* takes place in the historical periods of seventeenth century West Africa, colonial New England, an antebellum Louisiana plantation, and California after the Civil War. The male character, Doro, purchases two slaves, and Anyanwu, the heroine of the story and Doro's companion, makes sure that they are treated better than the other slaves because they are her "descendants" (87). The fact that the two main characters of this novel are "immortal" brings out the science fiction aspect of the novel" (78). Though the novel takes place in Africa for a limited time, an "African ethos dominates the whole book, indicating Butler's use of African American characters (78). In *Wild Seed,* Anyanwu is a dominant character with healing powers and in many ways is a model of African cultural values, as exemplified by her "sense of protection and her maternal instinct of care and concern for her people" (85). Govan claims that Butler uses Anyanwu to contribute to the underlying theme of kinship in *Wild Seed,* for the most important possession is the "well-being and safety of her kin" (85). Taking this theme a step further, Butler makes kinship the focus of the novel in *Kindred.* The historical setting of *Kindred* is nineteenth century Maryland and present-day California. The part of the story that takes place in nineteenth century Maryland is on a plantation with slave-holders. Dana, the heroine, finds herself "transversing time and geography" from present-day California to nineteenth century Maryland (88). She is psychically called by the slaveholder who will eventually be her great-grandfather, Rufus, when he is in danger, and returns home when she feels danger toward herself. Kinship becomes central to the novel once Dana figures out that Rufus is to become her great-grandfather. At this point, kinship becomes a responsibility for Dana. She must make sure that Rufus survives so that she saves her own existence. Again, the main character of this novel is an African American female who turns out to be the heroine.

Sandra Y. Govan does more than just superficially describe two of Butler's novels by probing deeper to show how they are alike and what particular points Butler is trying to make. For example, Govan successfully demonstrates how the historical novel, the slave narrative, and science fiction are brought together and in a unique new way treats traditional topics. Interestingly, Govan explains that Butler's writing is more important than just typical novels because Butler's novels educate people who might not otherwise be exposed to her type of writing in which sexual, racial, and historical issues are explored. She also points out that Butler's use of positive and heroic African American female main characters is necessary because it is generally lacking in contemporary science fiction. This point is important to include as it makes Octavia Butler's contributions in literature and society even more clear.

Rushdy, Ashraf H. A. "Families of Orphans: Relation and Disrelation in Octavia Butler's *Kindred.*" *College English* 55.2 (1993): 135-155.

In this work, Ashraf H. A. Rushdy explores the complex family and kinship themes in Octavia Butler's *Kindred*. Beginning with a brief summary of the time traveling situation of *Kindred*, Rushdy goes on to explain that the book is both a science fiction novel and a historical novel. He discusses in great detail how important Butler's use of "memory" is both to the historical aspect of the novel as well as to Dana, the main character of the story, in her understanding of her self-identity and the identity of her family. In his analysis of various passages from the novel, Rushdy attempts to explain how Dana's memory of her ancestory, which she actually takes place in and alters, is used to develop the essential theme of the family in *Kindred*.

In his discussion of this familial theme, Rushdy makes it clear that the "home" takes on a special meaning in *Kindred*. He says that it is "more than a place" in that it "signifies the liminal site where one can lose or reclaim a historically-defined modern self" (140).

Dana does successfully redefine herself, but is not without physical and spiritual sacrifices, such as when she physically loses her arm and continually risks her own existance, as Rushdy points out. Rushdy also shows that the home is important in understanding three of the main characters better because they each have a different meaning of that word in their lives: "For Dana, it marks the place between present relations with Kevin and past relations with Rufus. For Rufus, it marks ownership of property as different as the house and Dana. For Kevin, it marks the place where he and Dana can communicate" (140). According to Rushdy, a sense of family and home are based on Dana's "shared histories and collective memories" with other people just as much as they are based on blood ties (142). He states that this is central to the story in that in several instances, Dana chooses and relates more to her spiritual kindred, which are those who share "love and common experience" with her, over her blood relatives (155). Rushdy demonstrates that in reconstructing her family, Dana, who is actually an orphan, realizes that "her family is in the quarters and not in the big house; her sense of family is wrought from a common experience, and is not simply a matter of blood" (147).

In this article, Rushdy does a fairly complete job of explaining a difficult topic. In analyzing Butler's *Kindred,* he makes clear interpretations about Butler's views on the family and how its physical and spiritual realities relate to

Dana. He also supports all of his claims with evidence from the book, and his conclusions do seem valid. One shortcoming of this piece, however, is that, at times, Rushdy seems to be so involved in interpreting and analyzing the novel that he becomes confusing and hard to follow. An example of this is found in his explanation of the "memory" aspect of the novel. While he does spend a great amount of time discussing "memory" and its importance, this concept is still unclear and does not seem to be completely defined. But overall, Rushdy has produced an interesting article that is helpful in understanding the broader themes of the novel.

Salvaggio, Ruth. "Octavia Butler and the Black Science-Fiction Heroine." *Black American Literature Forum* 18.2 (1984): 78-81.

"Octavia Butler and the Black Science Fiction Heroine" is an article that discusses the importance of Octavia Butler's science fiction novels. There is an ongoing complaint that science fiction always revolves around male heroes. Butler is one of many women authors who is trying to change this by using "strong female protagonists" (78). According to Ruth Salvaggio, "What Butler has to offer is something very different" (78). Salvaggio explains that Butler's heroines are African American women who are put in situations where they face facism and sexism in future worlds. She makes her characters survive racial and sexual obstacles to achieve their independence. Salvaggio analyzes Butler's science fiction heroines in four of her novels: *Patternmaster, Mind of My Mind, Survivor,* and *Wild Seed.*

The first novel, *Patternmaster,* revolves around two brothers with one of them turning out to be the hero. Before the brother can become the hero, Amber, the heroine who has healing powers, must teach him how to defeat his brother. In the second novel, *Mind of My Mind,* the heroine, Mary, who has destructive and mental powers must kill her father, Doro to achieve her freedom. The third novel, *Survivor,* revolves mainly around the heroine Alanna, who has no powers at all. To survive, Alanna must no longer have beliefs in Christianity and must learn to compromise and survive in a "culture far from perfect" (80). The fourth novel, *Wild Seed,* is a prequel of the previous novels listed. The heroine of this novel is Anyanwu, a "healer," who has the power to change her physical appearance into various "creatures" (80). Her match is a male, Doro, who, like her, is immortal. Together they make a compromise realizing that they need each other for the companionship. Butler's heroines, as stated by Salvaggio "can tell us much about her science fiction precisely because they are the very core of that fiction" (81). One might expect the African female characters to s witch and take the role of the "male stereotype" of a hero or main character (81). Instead, these dangerous and powerful women are heroines because they "conquer the very notion of tyranny" by bringing healing and loving and showing a different kind of feminism (81) and heroism.

Ruth Salvaggio has written a satisfying article on Octavia Butler's science fiction heroines. Science fiction usually is written with males dominating the novel, and Salvaggio strongly demonstrates how Butler is changing this by making her characters strong, independent females. Salvaggio stays clearly focused on the heroines of Butler's writings throughout her article, and, in doing so, she offers a better understanding of how and why Butler uses African American women as her main characters.

Student Sample Annotated Bibliography: History

Annotated Bibliography Project Cover Sheet

Project Title: __Baseball and American Culture__

Course: __History 1B__

Name: __Taidgh Simpson__

Date: __July 11, 1994__

Bennett, Jay. "Touching All Bases" *The Economist,* February 1993, pp. 110–115

Jay Bennett writes this article on the recent realignment in Major League baseball and the inter-division play that is sure to follow. When the change from having divisions in each league to having three divisions in each league took place, baseball purists everywhere lamented the decision. One of the oldest traditions in baseball was being changed simply to try to make baseball more exciting. Now that changes are being made, this would be a perfect time to make another.

As it is now, realignment has already made a major change in baseball. What Bennett is arguing for is inter-league play. Not only would this allow fans to see stars from the other leagues, but it would also give the players the chance to play the best players in the majors, and not just the best players in their league. The best way to make this work would be to have each team play each team from the other league three times. The one big problem with the inter-league play, the use of the designated hitter in the American league, could be solved in the same way as it is in the World Series: the home teams' rules apply. And as for the argument that it would make the World Series less interesting, says Bennett, there seems no shortage of viewers for the Super Bowl or the NBA Finals.

The reader tends to agree with Mr. Bennett, but has to doubt that the reformation would come about any time soon. His arguments are all well thought out and are also all valid. However, the prospect of inter-league play, although reasonable sounding, comes too close to the change in the alignment of the leagues and therefore will not come around anytime soon.

Bluthardt, Robert F. "Fenway Park and the Golden Age of the Baseball Park, 1909-1915." *Journal of Popular Culture,* March 1987, pp. 43–52.

In this article, Robert Bluthardt explains the motivations behind the construction of thirteen new baseball parks in a six year period, 1909–1915. Boston, Brooklyn, Detroit, Chicago, and Pittsburgh were the most extravagant of all the new stadiums. Because baseball had become such mainstay in society, better stadiums were needed for the increasing amount of fans that were flocking to watch the game.

This article goes on to state that these new parks were built for four reasons: attendance, accessibility, better playing conditions, and safer conditions in the ballpark. Fans that wanted to see baseball games were pleased by the changes. More seats were made available (in some cases, the number of seats was doubled or even tripled) and these seats were much more luxurious than those in the older stadiums. Seats were now made of concrete and steel, thus eliminating the dangers of having wooden bleachers and allowing patrons increased security. To insure crowd management, turnstiles were constructed, limiting access of fans to areas other than their own. Many stadiums, like Ebbets Field and Fenway Park, were placed near to subways and streets, thus allowing maximum availability. Also, the field area was expanded while other field conditions were also improved. Advertisements were removed from the outfield walls and visiting locker rooms were installed, thus allowing privacy for the players. Expensive changes that were not always appreciated were made. Opulent chandeliers and scoreboards were put in, thus increasing the allure of the ballpark. These new and improved ballpark often increased the values of the surrounding areas, thus earning the endorsements of city mayors, councilmen, and other local officials.

This article effectively explained the reasoning behind the building of stadiums in the early 20th century. Bluthardt's article also explains the features of each baseball park and how each ballpark was outfitted with its own special features. His article fully explains the movement to improve baseball and make it more appealing to fans of all ages.

Bruggink, Thomas H. and Rose Jr., David R. "Financial Restraint in the Free Agent Labor Market for Major League baseball: Payers Look at Strike Three" *Southern Economic Journal*. October 1990, pp. 1029–43.

David Rose and Thomas Bruggink have written this article about the problem over free agency between the baseball players and the owners. They contend that the principal issues have been "salaries, the player pension fund, and the negotiating opportunities of players who are classified as free agents." This feud has led to many law suits and court dates, while the relationship between the owners and the players has slowly soured. Baseball players have been encouraged to give way to the owners' wishes but have elected to fight the unfair (by their standards) regulations.

Professional baseball has become a primary source of data for many economists. Pay levels and revenue statistics are easily measured, supporting an economist's claims. In 1987, when baseball arbitrator Thomas Roberts ruled that baseball owners were guilty of collusion in the free agent market, the biggest issue in the disagreement was decided in favor of the players. Thomas Roberts said that baseball team owners did not bid on free agent players for the 1985 season, thus forcing the player to stay with his former team and keeping the salaries of players down. This decision started the players back on the road to recovery in what had become a biased situation in favor of the owners. for years and years, owners had been doing this sort of things to keep the money in their own pockets. Since the beginning of free agency, the salaries of the free agent players had been rising. Teams were willing to pay a lot of money in order to gain a player to help in their quest for a pennant. The result was a bidding war in which the owner who received the player was forced to pay a substantially higher salary. The owners felt that they were being conspired against and so, conspired, themselves, against the players. Now, with the support of the arbitration, the players can strike back. This struggle for power will be a see-saw battle and will not end until a salary cap and a collective bargaining agreement is made, conclude the authors: "The owners and players must work out some compromises on the free agency system to prevent a third strike by the players."

Bruggink and Rose are right on target with their analysis. Although this article was written in 1990, their predictions have become facts, as, today, a strike threatens to obliterate the second half of the 1994 season. The reader agrees with everything that the authors said, because all that they say is true.

Higgins, George V. "Fields of Broken Dreams." *The American Scholar.* May 1990, pp. 199–210.

George Higgins' "Fields of Broken Dreams" focuses on the banishment of Pete Rose, the extenuating circumstances surrounding his suspension for life, Rose's friends, and has examined the mind and persona of the person who exiled him, A. Bartlett Giamatti, one of the greatest commissioners in the history of baseball.

Not only was Giamatti well liked and respected in the baseball community, but he was also an accomplished professor at Yale, a history buff and an avid Red Sox fan. He was thought of as a perfect fit for the position of baseball commissioner. However, with one decision he affected the life off millions of fans and one of the biggest legends of all time. In 1989, just eight days before his tragic death, Pete Rose was "invited" to the commissioners office to confer in New York. Giamatti was talking to the most recognizable and most colorful player on the Big Red Machine of the 70's. As a result of this meeting, Rose was "suspended from baseball for life" (later, in a subsequent investigation by the federal government, Rose w as sentenced to jail for tax evasion).

Betting on baseball was especially dangerous because of the implications it contained. If Peter Rose was betting on baseball while managing, that meant that Rose theoretically changed lineups, pitchers, etc. at whim in order to balance his books. This dangerous possibility meant that Giamatti's beloved game was being jeopardized for the benefit of one of its beneficiaries: Rose. The only solution, whether right or wrong was to remove the problem, which is one thing that Giamatti did quickly, in the form of permanently suspending Pete Rose, even if he was an intrinsic part of baseball history.

Higgin's clear and incredibly detailed information on the surrounding elements in the Rose banishment appeal to the reader and give his thoughts credibility. Higgins style is direct, appealing to many readers and allowing the reader to stay on the same level as Higgins. Regardless of the pesonal feelings and prejudices of the reader about Rose, Higgins is able to constuct an informative paper while at the same time let his opinions be known.

Singell Jr., Larry D. "Baseball-Specific Human Capital: Why Good but Not Great Players Are More Likely to Coach in the Major Leagues." *Southern Economic Journal.* September 1991, pp. 77–86.

In this article, Larry Singell argues that a vast majority of Major League managers were fair baseball players, and not stars in the game. This argument is based on polls of former players and their decision on whether or not to coach in baseball based on their potential earnings. Many former baseball players have become managers after they have retired from playing the game. Yogi Berra, Joe Torre, and Rogers Hornsby are some such managers and all but Berra and Hornsby were average players. However, in baseball, as in other sports, the players that become coaches were, most likely, average players at best.

Many hypothesi have been developed about why this is so. One theory is that superstar players lose patience easily with lesser skilled players and therefore are harder on them and not are not as fair to them. A ex-superstar is likely to say something like "why can't they play as well as I did?" Another theory is that lesser skilled players work harder and thus learn the game more thoroughly. Through hard work, average players learn basic skills needed for baseball and can therefore apply the skills and pass them on easier. The last major theory is that lesser players, while sitting on the bench, have more time and are more inclined to look at baseball more closely than a player who is participating and does not really have time to watch.

Larry Singell uses many statistics and formulas to explain his hypothesi. Although hard to understand at times, Singell presents his ideas clearly. Also, through his extensive use of formulas, Singell proves his ideas to be correct, if the reader takes the time to sort through the confusing amount of numbers and statistics and "crunch" them into an equation.

Project Registration Form

In order to avoid duplication of topics and/or research, your professor may require you to register your annotated bibliography topic. You may also be asked to provide several citations so that your professor may chart your progress. If this is the case, use this project registration form.

Student Name:_____

Course:_____

Project Topic:_____

Proposed Representative Sources:

1._____

_____

2._____

_____

3._____

_____